Photographic Theory
for the Motion Picture Cameraman

In the same
Screen Textbooks Series
edited by Russell Campbell
produced by The Tantivy Press

PRACTICAL MOTION PICTURE PHOTOGRAPHY

compiled and edited by Russell Campbell

Forthcoming
DIRECTING MOTION PICTURES
LIGHTING FOR MOTION PICTURES
MOTION PICTURE CAMERAS
MOTION PICTURE CAMERA OPERATING

in association with The London Film School

SCREEN TEXTBOOKS

Photographic Theory for the Motion Picture Cameraman

Compiled and edited by
Russell Campbell

Series Consultant E. Smith-Morris
Vice-Principal, London Film School

A. Zwemmer Limited, London
A.S. Barnes & Co., Inc., San Diego • New York

Cover and graphics by
Michael Hoad and Stefan Dreja

Third Printing 1981

FIRST PUBLISHED 1970
© 1970 by Russell Campbell
Library of Congress Catalogue Card No.: 73-125885
SBN: 302 02067 5 (U.K.)
ISBN: 0-498-07776-4 (U.S.)

Printed in the United States of America

Contents

Preface and Acknowledgements

Photographic Theory for the Motion Picture Cameraman and its companion volume, *Practical Motion Picture Photography,* are the first books in a series which, it is hoped, will eventually extend to all aspects of professional film-making. The topics dealt with in these two books are thus selected with a view to the area which will be covered in future texts, in particular those devoted to cameras, camera operating and lighting.

The method adopted in compiling the books has been that of consultation with the appropriate experts within the film industry, and I am extremely indebted to the many individuals and firms without whose generous co-operation the work could not have been undertaken. Such support goes a long way towards ensuring that the "Screen Textbooks" Series will be as accurate and up-to-the-minute as possible, and I hope that the books may, in return, be of service to the industry as well as to students desiring, one day, to enter it.

Photographic Theory for the Motion Picture Cameraman is designed for readers approaching the subject for the first time, although some acquaintance with the elements of photography, film-making or television gained through practical experience would be an advantage. More abstruse scientific and technological considerations have been purposely avoided. A basic knowledge of mathematics, physics and chemistry is assumed, but this should be no more than that which is provided by a general secondary school education.

Among those who assisted with the preparation of the book I would particularly like to thank Mr. R. F. Ebbetts, A.R.P.S., F.B.K.S., Managing Director of Filmatic Laboratories Ltd., for his invaluable advice on all aspects of laboratory practice, and Mr Robin Carpenter, M.B.K.S., of the Motion Picture Division, Kodak Ltd., for his wealth of information concerning film stocks and their use. Several firms contributed material relating to their branch of the industry and in some cases checked the relevant portions of the manuscript. In this connection I would especially like to acknowledge the help of the Macbeth Instrument Corporation of Newburgh, New York; Metro/Kalvar Inc. of Connecticut; and the Eastman Kodak Company of Rochester, New York. Mr. L. B. Happé, F.B.K.S., F.R.P.S., Technical Manager of Technicolor Ltd, was of great assistance in the preparation of the sections dealing with Technicolor processes. The approach adopted in several chapters was suggested by lectures given by Mr. Phil Mottram at the London Film School (formerly the London School of Film Technique), to whom I would also like to express my thanks.

There are few books devoted to motion picture photographic theory as such. For the black-and-white sections, I found Leslie J. Wheeler's *Principles of Cinematography* and D. J. Corbett's *Motion Picture and Television Film* very helpful, and for the chapters on colour photography and the requirements of film for television transmission I am particularly indebted to the work of Dr. R. W. G. Hunt and Dr. Boris Townsend. The chief books and periodicals consulted are listed in the bibliography.

The manuscript was kindly read by Mr. Baynham Honri, F.B.K.S., F.R.P.S., F.R.S.A., B.S.C., Technical Consultant to the Rank Film Production Division, whose long experience with every aspect of the film industry made his comments particularly pertinent and valuable. In the United States, Dr. Raymond Fielding, author of *The Technique of Special-Effects Cinematography,* and Professor Hollis Todd, co-author of *Photographic Sensitometry,* generously checked the manuscript for usages unfamiliar to American readers and made a wide variety of other suggestions for improvements which I was most happy to incorporate. Responsibility for any obscurities or errors which remain is, however, entirely my own.

For their constant assistance and longstanding patience I would like to thank Mr. Michael Hoad, who drew the diagrams, and Mr. Stefan Dreja, who designed the cover. Both are responsible for the typography and layout. For other illustrations I am indebted to Bell and Howell Ltd., Filmatic Laboratories Ltd., Kodak Ltd., the Macbeth Instrument Corporation, Metro/Kalvar Inc., the Rank Organisation, SOS Photo-Cine-Optics Inc. and Technicolor Ltd.

Finally, I would like to thank Mr. Robert Dunbar, Principal of the London Film School, who initiated the project; Mr. Peter Cowie, Director of the Tantivy Press, whose continual encouragement ensured that it would reach completion; and especially Mr. E. Smith-Morris, Vice-Principal of the London Film School, who proposed the allocation of topics between the various books in the series, suggested contacts, read each chapter of the manuscript as it was completed, made comments which were invariably just and relevant, and in general supervised the writing in the best possible manner.

I would like to point out that the terms used and practices referred to are those common in Great Britain and the United States. Phenidone, Technicolor, Eastman, Kodak, Agfa and (in some countries) Metol are Registered Trade Marks.

R. C.

Chapter I
Introduction to the Photographic Process

Photography is a method of producing images by exposing sensitive material to the chemical action of light. Since light plays a vital role in the process, it is appropriate to begin this study with a short analysis of its somewhat complex physical behaviour.

The Nature of Light

Light is a form of energy. It may be converted by either natural or artificial means into other energy forms, which include heat and chemical, electrical and mechanical energy. The conversion to chemical energy, known as the photochemical effect, is the basis of photography; the photothermal effect (conversion to heat) and the photo-electric effect are also important.

The transmission of light has been understood both as the excitation of a stream of particles (a theory first propounded by Newton) and as a wave motion (as suggested by Huygens). Newton's hypothesis suffered from bad repute until the development of quantum theory in the Twentieth century revindicated it—in a rather modified form. Quantum mechanics explains light as consisting of a stream of particles of zero mass (or more precisely zero rest-mass) known as *photons,* which are analogous to the elementary particles of matter such as electrons and neutrons. The probability that the photons making up a given beam of light will move in certain ways is described by a mathematical equation of the simple sine-wave type: this is said to account for behaviour such as refraction which gave rise to the older moving-wave theories of the nature of light. It is still convenient, however, to speak of light "waves."

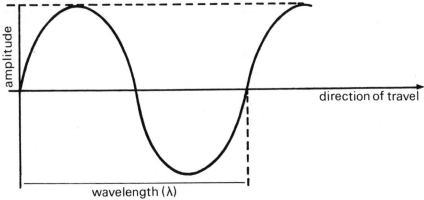

Fig. 1.1. Typical waveform characteristics

The Electromagnetic Spectrum

Waveform properties may be illustrated by a diagram such as Fig. 1.1. *Amplitude* is defined as the vertical distance between the peak of the curve

9

and the horizontal axis; *wavelength* (λ) as the linear distance occupied by a complete wave or *cycle,* measured horizontally; while *frequency* (f) is defined as the number of such cycles occurring per second. The *speed* or *velocity* (v) of such a wave transmission is the product of its wavelength and frequency, thus

$$\lambda \times f = v$$

The *electromagnetic spectrum* is a continuum of electromagnetic radiation consisting of photons with waveform properties of this type. Electromagnetic energy is radiated at a constant speed of 186,000 miles per second (or 3×10^8 metres per second), designated by the letter c. Thus the wavelength of any form of electromagnetic energy varies inversely with its frequency, and all such forms may be arrayed in a continuous spectrum, ranging from gamma rays with wavelengths of the order of 10^{-15} metres to low-frequency radio transmissions with wavelengths of some 10^6 metres. The boundaries between different forms of radiation are not distinct and overlapping occurs. Light, or visible radiation, occupies a small portion of this total spectrum, sandwiched between ultra-violet and infra-red rays (see Fig. 1.2).

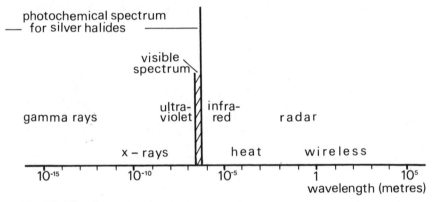

Fig. 1.2. The electromagnetic spectrum

The wavelength of light is normally measured in terms of a unit equal to one-millionth of a millimetre (or 10^{-9} metre), known as the millimicron (mμ) or—which is to be preferred—the nanometre (nm): the visible spectrum ranges from approximately 400nm to 700nm. Differences of wavelength within this band are perceived by the eye as changes in colour, varying from violet and blue (at the 400nm end of the spectrum) through green and yellow to red (at the 700nm end). White light from a source such as the sun is a mixture of the colours of the visible spectrum in approximately equal proportions: it may be analysed into its component colours by means of a device such as a prism. The rainbow is a natural visible spectrum.

The gradation of colours within the spectrum is continuous. The "seven colours of the rainbow" commonly enumerated derive essentially from Newton's predilection for the mystic number. By varying one's terminology, the spectrum may be divided into smaller or larger segments: in colour photography, for instance, there are three simple divisions of blue, green and red.

10

The Sensitivity Range of Photographic Emulsions

Fig. 1.2. also illustrates the sensitivity range to electromagnetic radiation of the normal panchromatic film emulsion as compared with that of the human eye. This is known as the *photochemical spectrum* for silver halides, and as may be seen includes gamma rays, X-rays and ultra-violet rays in addition to visible light. Several practical implications arise from this broader range of photographic materials:

(a) Film stock is gradually exposed by gamma rays which have penetrated the earth's atmosphere. This raises the *fog level* of the emulsion and accounts for the dating on film stocks.

(b) Because X-rays also fog ordinary film stock, it is important to beware of X-ray checks at customs, for example.

(c) Ultra-violet radiation is recorded as haze on monochrome stocks and as excessive blue in colour. Ultra-violet rays are most concentrated at high altitudes and near certain reflecting surfaces such as the sea; when photographing in this type of location it is necessary to guess at their existence and use appropriate filters.

Given special treatment, photographic emulsions may also be made sensitive to infra-red radiation. Special effects such as night shots are made feasible in this way, since physical objects absorb and reflect infra-red rays in a different manner from light. Further possibilities arise from the superior haze penetrating power of infra-red rays, which are longer in wavelength than rays of the visible spectrum, and therefore enable ultra-long-distance shots to be made.

The Behaviour of Light

Within a given medium, light travels in straight lines: this phenomenon is known as *rectilinear propagation.* When light strikes the surface of another medium it may be *reflected,* i.e. bounced back into the original medium; *transmitted,* i.e. propagated through the new medium at an angle determined by the angle of incidence and the relative densities of the two media; or *absorbed,* i.e. converted by the new medium into another form of energy, such as heat.

The illumination of a surface is termed *specular,* if light travels directly from the source or sources and thus strikes the surface at a single angle, or a few distinct angles at most, e.g. sunlight; it is termed *diffuse* if as a result of scattering by an intermediate medium light reaches the surface from a wide variety of angles, e.g. light from a blue or overcast sky.

Reflection

Reflection, like illumination, may be specular or diffuse.

(a) *Specular (Mirror) Reflection.* If a ray of light (a *ray* is defined as a beam of zero width) strikes a surface whose irregularities are small compared with the wavelength of light, specular reflection will occur (see Fig. 1.3). The ray will be reflected about the normal (or line perpendicular to the surface) so that the angle of incidence equals the angle of reflection; the incident ray, the normal and the reflected ray will all lie in one plane. Since specular reflection is extremely efficient, very little absorption occurs, and thus (in the case of non-metallic surfaces) there will be no colour change in the reflected ray (see *Absorption*): white light is reflected as white light; a mirror has no colour of its own. Other examples of specular reflectors are

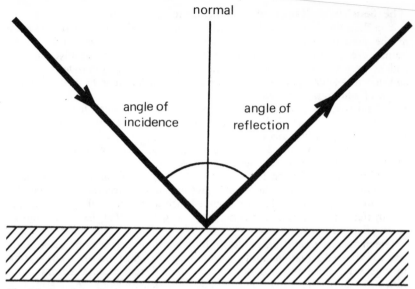

normal

angle of incidence

angle of reflection

Fig. 1.3. Specular reflection

aluminium foil and polished stainless steel.

(b) *Diffuse (Scattered) Reflection.* When the irregularities of a surface are large compared with the wavelength of light, diffuse reflection will occur (see Fig. 1.4). A ray striking a diffuse surface will be split up and reflected equally in all directions. Generally, a much higher proportion of incident light will be absorbed by a diffuse reflector than by a specular reflector, although certain substances such as magnesium oxide (MgO) have highly efficient diffuse reflecting surfaces.

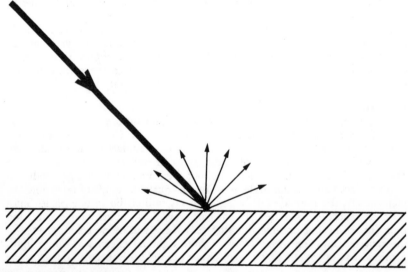

Fig. 1.4. Diffuse reflection

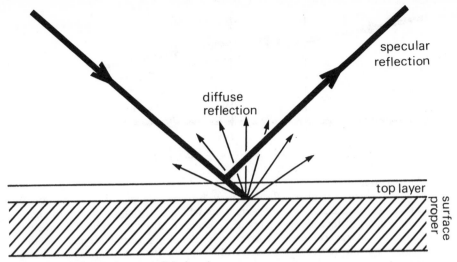

Fig. 1.5. Reflection from a polished surface

(c) *Partial (Mixed) Reflection.* The reflecting characteristics of most surfaces are a mixture of the specular and diffuse types. Special considerations arise in the case of polished surfaces, such as varnished wood, or wet surfaces. In such instances light is reflected specularly from the top layer, the polish or water, and diffusely from the surface proper. This effect may have applications for colour photography. Normally, in the case of a partially reflecting surface, light reflected diffusely and thus usually coloured (see *Absorption*) is mixed with white light from specular reflection: the colour of the surface is thus made less vivid or, technically speaking, *desaturated*. If, however, the surface is polished or wetted and then viewed at an angle to avoid specular reflections, the rays of white and coloured light will be separated and the colour of the surface will appear more vivid—there will be an increase in saturation. This is illustrated in Fig. 1.5. For related reasons, the colour of a surface appears more saturated if the illumination of it is specular, i.e. strongly directional, rather than diffuse, provided the surface is viewed from a suitable angle.

Refraction

The laws of refraction describe the behaviour of light which is bent as it passes from one medium to another of different optical density. Refraction is of crucial importance in lens and camera design but has little application to the photographic topics discussed in this book. It is sufficient perhaps to note that in the case of light passing through a parallel-sided medium, such as a film or filter, refraction which occurs at the first surface is counteracted by that which occurs at the second surface, and thus deviation does not occur. Rays of light striking the medium at an angle other than the normal will however be slightly displaced (see Fig. 1.6). This is the reason for the focussing adjustments which are necessary when filters are inserted between the lens and the film plane, as is the practice with certain cameras. For most other practical purposes the effect may be discounted provided the medium is sufficiently thin.

13

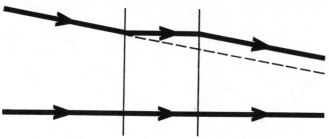

Fig. 1.6. Transmission through a transparent parallel-sided medium

Absorption

Light which is neither reflected nor transmitted upon striking a surface is said to be absorbed. Now the extent to which a surface will absorb light falling upon it depends partly upon the wavelength of the light. Thus a surface may appear coloured by selectively absorbing certain regions of the spectrum while reflecting others. A blue object, for example, absorbs light from the green and red regions of the spectrum (i.e. wavelengths higher than about 500nm): illuminated in red light, it will look black. Objects which absorb light equally from all parts of the spectrum appear white, grey or black in white light.

An opaque surface which absorbs only a small portion of the light falling on it is said to have a high *reflection factor* or *reflectance,* defined as the ratio between light reflected from the surface and the corresponding incident light, expressed as a percentage or decimal value. This factor is of considerable importance in lighting and exposure control. Typical approximate reflectances are:

> Fresh snow...............95%
> White cartridge paper.......80%
> Face highlight (white)......35%
> Brickwork................12%
> Black velvet.............. 3%

These are examples of diffuse reflectors: coefficients for specular reflectors are naturally of a high order. The average reflectance of a diffuse surface is approximately 18%.

The Measurement of Light

The two characteristics of a light source most commonly measured are its intensity and its spectral, or colour, composition. The measurement of light intensity is known as *photometry;* spectral composition is measured by a system called (somewhat misleadingly) *colour temperature.*

Photometry

The intensity of a light source may be measured either as it is incident to, or as it is reflected from a surface. *Luminous intensity* and *illumination* are systems for measuring incident light, while reflected light is measured in units of *luminance.* The term *brightness* is sometimes found in place of luminance, but because of its lack of precision this usage is to be avoided.

Luminous intensity is a system of units whereby the light emitted from a source is measured by comparison with a standard source. The international standard now adopted is the *candela* (cd), which differs little from the older *standard candle*. Thus the luminous intensity of a lamp or other light source is frequently quoted in *candlepower*.

The *illumination* of, or light falling upon, a given surface depends on
(a) the luminous intensity of the source
(b) in the case of a lamp, the optical system employed
(c) the distance between the source and the surface
(d) the absorption of the medium through which the light travels (haze, etc.)
(e) the angle of incidence of the light source with respect to the surface.

The unit of illumination is defined as the illumination of a surface all points of which are 1 foot (or 1 metre) distant from a uniform point source of 1 candela, and is called the *foot-candle* (or in the metric system, the metre-candle or *lux*). Incident light meters are normally calibrated in foot-candles or lux. 1 foot-candle is equal to 10.764 lux. Illumination may also occasionally be expressed in *lumens per square foot,* units identical to the foot-candle.

The *inverse square law* describes the relationship between the illumination of a surface and its distance from a given light source. Other factors being disregarded, the illumination of a surface is inversely proportional to the square distance from the source, assuming that it is a point source suspended remotely from reflecting surfaces. If devices such as lamp reflectors are used in order to concentrate light into a beam, the inverse square law is modified and illumination will depend also on the beam position and beam setting of the lamp.

The illumination of a surface is at a maximum when the light falls at right angles to the surface, i.e. the *angle of incidence* is zero. At any other angle illumination will be less (proportional to the cosine of the angle of incidence) (see Fig. 1.7).

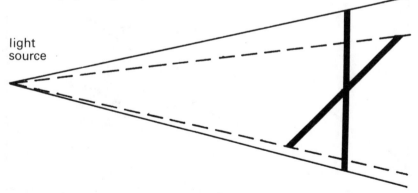

light source

Fig. 1.7. Effect of angle of incidence on the illumination of a surface

Luminance is a measure of the light reflected from a given surface. This depends upon
(a) the incident illumination
(b) the reflectance of the surface

(c) the manner in which reflection takes place, i.e. the extent to which the surface is a diffuse or specular reflector

(d) in the case of specular reflectors, the angle from which the measurement is taken.

In the non-metric system, luminance may be measured either in *foot-lamberts* or in *candles per square foot*. A foot-lambert is defined as the amount of light reflected by a perfectly diffuse surface with 100% reflectance, when the surface has an illumination of one foot-candle and is at right angles to the light source, i.e. where total incident light equals total reflected light. A candles per square foot value is obtained by dividing the foot-lambert value by π, a measure which is taken to allow for the hemispherical nature of diffuse reflection. For a perfectly diffuse surface, the luminance (L), in candles per square foot, is therefore given by the formula

$$L = \frac{IR}{\pi}$$

where I is the illumination in foot-candles and R the reflectance of the surface. The metric equivalent of the candles per square foot measurement is the candela per square metre or *nit*.

Most professional reflected light meters are calibrated in candles per square foot, while others use arbitrary light values for use on a calculator incorporated with the meter. It should be noted that luminance may also be used as a measure of an extended light source, such as a fluorescent tube.

Colour Temperature

The colour composition of various "white" light sources varies considerably. Tungsten light, for example, is considerably yellower than light from

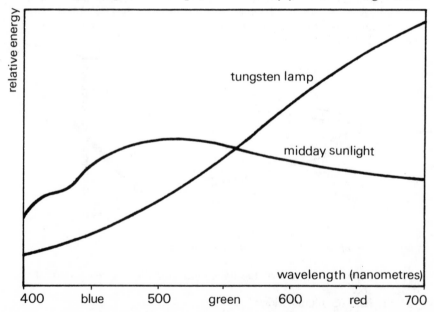

Fig. 1.8. Relative spectral energy curves of a tungsten lamp and average midday sunlight

16

the sun at midday, as is shown by the respective spectral energy curves in Fig. 1.8. Human eyesight has self-adjusting mechanisms to compensate for such differences, and thus we may scarcely notice changes in the colour composition of ambient light; such changes, however, are vitally important in colour photography.

The exact spectral composition of a light source may be given only by a detailed analysis of its energy output at many different wavelengths. For photography and related purposes, however, a simplified system has been devised, known as *colour temperature*. This system is based on the fact that many sources emit light as a consequence of being heated. The energy emitted by an object which is gradually heated will be composed, at first, entirely of infra-red radiation and heat waves, and will then include ever-increasing proportions of visible light (see Fig. 1.9). Since visible light is radiated first at the red end of the spectrum, the ratio of blue to red light emitted by the radiating body will increase as the temperature of the body rises. The mixture of light emitted at various temperatures will be found to

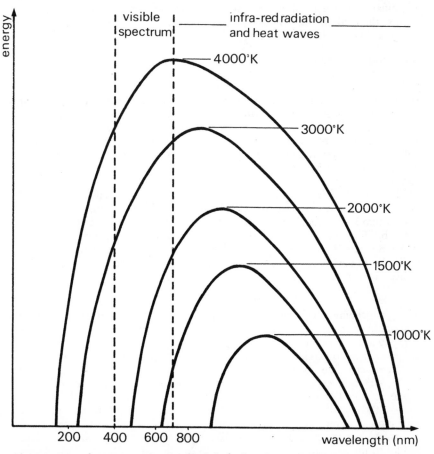

Fig. 1.9. Spectral energy curves of a black body heated to various temperatures

reproduce roughly the composition of various daylight and artificial light sources, and this provides a convenient method of measurement.

Colour temperature is defined as that temperature to which a full radiator, or *black body,* would have to be raised for it to emit light which will visually match that of the source being measured. The temperature is quoted in degrees Kelvin, a scale whose units are identical to degrees Centigrade but in which zero is set at —273°C., or absolute zero. The comparative colour temperature of various light sources is given on p. 139.

It is important to note that colour temperature applies only to continuous-spectrum light sources. Sodium and mercury vapour lamps, for example, have a spectral distribution of a completely different nature from that of an incandescent black body, while fluorescent tubes emit light which is only partly of the continuous-spectrum type (see Fig. 1.10). The concept of colour temperature is therefore most useful for tungsten sources.

A *photo-electric colour temperature meter* may be used to measure the colour balance of a continuous-spectrum light source. Such meters measure illumination independently through red and blue filters (on elaborate instruments, three filters are employed) and compare the values obtained. They are generally calibrated in degrees Kelvin.

The Photographic Process

The technique of throwing an image on to a screen by means of a pinhole or lens system in a device such as a camera obscura has been known for many centuries. Photography consists of capturing such an image by exploiting the photochemical effect. Certain substances are *light-sensitive,* that is they undergo chemical change when exposed to light. Salts of metallic silver are particularly light-sensitive, and of these three halides—silver bromide, silver chloride and silver iodide—are the most useful for photographic processes. The basic method by which they may be made to create a permanent black-and-white image is as follows.

First, an *emulsion* is prepared, consisting of grains of silver halide suspended in a solution of gelatin. This is then coated on to a support, in most cases a film base, and placed in the focal plane of the camera. *Exposure* takes place by allowing light from the subject, focussed by the lens system, to strike the emulsion, usually very briefly. The degree of exposure depends upon the intensity of the light and the time it is allowed to operate in the camera, and is thus defined:

$$\text{Exposure} = \text{Intensity} \times \text{Time}$$

The photochemical effect of a short exposure with light of a high intensity is roughly equivalent, over a limited range, to the effect of a long exposure with light of a proportionately lower intensity, but for extreme values of either variable the relationship does not hold good, a phenomenon known as *Reciprocity Law Failure.*

The effect of exposure to light is to reduce minute quantities of silver halide to metallic silver. These particles of silver form as specks on the silver halide grains, their distribution depending on the amount of light reaching each point: thus a *latent image* is formed. The film is then placed in a *developer* which has the effect, like light, of chemically reducing silver halides to metallic silver, but which is very much faster. During this process those halide grains which have been previously exposed to light, and thus

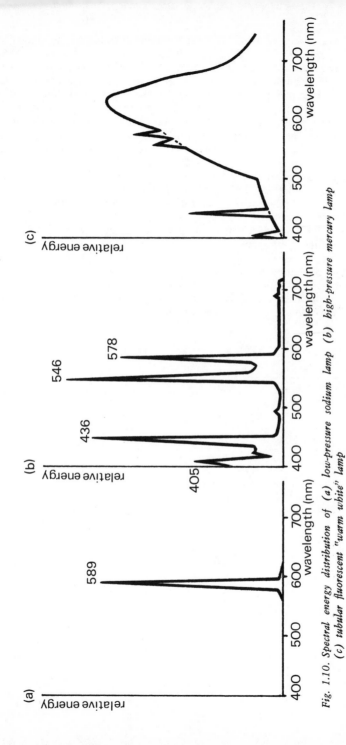

Fig. 1.10. Spectral energy distribution of (a) low-pressure sodium lamp (b) high-pressure mercury lamp (c) tubular fluorescent "warm white" lamp

19

already have specks of metallic silver on their surface, are developed very much more quickly than others. Thus by controlling the time and temperature of development the latent image may be converted to a visible *negative* image, in which highlights of the original scene are represented by concentrations of black metallic silver. As the unconverted silver halide grains are still sensitive to light, it is next necessary to *fix* the image by immersing the film in a silver halide solvent such as sodium thiosulphate. After washing and drying, the film, now bearing a permanent negative image, may be used to produce a *positive* image by shining light through it on to material coated with a similar emulsion and processed in the same manner. This procedure is called *printing,* and the number of prints which may be taken from a single negative is limited only by physical wear and tear.

Colour photography utilises a sophisticated adaptation of this fundamental process in order to produce images consisting of superimposed dye layers. In the layout of this book, Chapters Two to Seven inclusive deal solely with black-and-white photography except where otherwise indicated; Chapters Eight to Eleven are devoted to colour; while Chapter Twelve is applicable to any type of motion picture filming for the ultimate purpose of television transmission. While some of the material may be found to apply to photography in general, it should be understood that the text throughout refers specifically to motion picture films and processes.

Chapter II
Film Stock

Motion picture film stock consists of one or more emulsion layers coated on to a transparent film base, usually with the addition of other layers for special purposes.

A. THE PHOTOGRAPHIC EMULSION

The Binder

The silver halide grains, or micro-crystals, which are the light-sensitive components of standard photographic emulsions, are insoluble in water. Thus silver halide which is formed by precipitation in the absence of any other medium will coagulate into a creamy curd, and in this form is quite unsuitable for spreading evenly on to a support material. This means that it is necessary to employ a substance, known as a *binder,* which will effectively disperse the grains of halide as they are formed and ensure that they adhere permanently to the support. The substance used for this purpose is *gelatin,* an organic compound belonging to the protein group which is extracted from bones and hide clippings of cows and pigs. Discovered in 1871, gelatin has since remained unrivalled as a binder despite intensive scientific research.

The Properties of Gelatin

The virtues of gelatin are many.

(a) It is a viscous protective *colloid,* or suspension of minute semi-solid particles, and not only prevents coagulation but also provides a medium in which the size of halide grains may be controlled during the manufacturing process.

(b) It does not react with chemicals used during the development and fixing stages, and is chemically stable with time.

(c) It prevents, or at the least drastically retards, the reduction of unexposed halide crystals by becoming *adsorbed* to their surface (i.e. condensed in the form of a film), thus creating a protective barrier.

(d) It also helps the process of development by acting as a *halogen acceptor* (*halogens* are the closely related group of elements—bromine, chlorine, iodine etc.—corresponding to the halides). The bromine, for example, liberated by the reduction of silver bromide to metallic silver would re-combine (in the dark) with atoms of silver if it was not prevented by the action of gelatin from doing so.

(e) An important subsidiary characteristic is that it contains certain very powerful *sensitising agents* in the form of sulphide impurities which become adsorbed to the surface of halide grains during emulsion manufacture (see *After-ripening*) and greatly increase the film sensitivity (or *speed*).

(f) At normal temperatures it takes the state of a tough jelly or *gel,* but when heated in water above 30°C. (86°F.) it readily dissolves into a solution (sometimes called a *sol*) suitable for coating, and this process is easily reversible.

(g) It is permeable: when placed in cold water it swells, without disintegrating or dissolving, and is then easily penetrated by chemical developers, etc.

(h) When dry, it is tough, strong and durable, securing the crystals of silver halide in position and protecting them from damage by abrasion. It may also be hardened by agents such as chrome alum or formalin.

(i) It is transparent.

(j) It is cheap, easily obtainable and may be manufactured in bulk to specific standards.

Choice of Halides

The halides chosen for a particular emulsion depend upon the purpose for which the emulsion is designed. Silver chloride, alone or in combination with bromide, is in common use for certain types of printing papers in still photography, but its application in motion picture work is confined to some colour printing stocks (see Chapter Ten), when its insensitivity to blue light can be exploited to good advantage. Silver bromide, being more sensitive to light in general and to the blue region of the spectrum in particular, is otherwise universally adopted in the motion picture industry, for both negative and positive film. It is often used in conjunction with a small proportion, up to 5%, of silver iodide, which though unsuitable for use on its own considerably increases the speed of bromide emulsions when employed in small amounts.

Emulsification

Silver halide may be formed by direct combination of metallic silver and a halogen, so that the reaction is of the type

$$Ag \quad + \quad Br \quad \rightarrow \quad AgBr$$
$$\text{silver} \qquad \text{bromine} \qquad \text{silver bromide}$$

The method employed in the regular production of photographic emulsions, however, involves the mixture of solutions in an emulsion "kettle." Metallic silver is first dissolved in dilute nitric acid to form silver nitrate, which is then placed in solution with water. A solution of an alkali (e.g. potassium) halide is then mixed with the silver nitrate solution in the presence of gelatin and a double decomposition reaction takes place:

$$AgNO_3 \quad + \quad KBr \quad \rightarrow \quad AgBr \quad + \quad KNO_3$$
$$\text{silver nitrate} \qquad \text{potassium bromide} \qquad \text{silver bromide} \qquad \text{potassium nitrate}$$

Silver bromide, being insoluble, is *precipitated,* but the presence of gelatin prevents the crystals formed from coagulating and they are distributed evenly, forming a suspension or (as it is commonly known) emulsion.

Certain emulsification processes use ammonia, which tends to increase sensitivity. In this case silver ammoniate is generally employed instead of silver nitrate:

$$Ag(NH_3)_2NO_3 + KBr \quad \rightarrow \quad AgBr \quad + \quad KNO_3 \quad + \quad 2NH_3$$
$$\text{silver} \qquad \text{potassium} \qquad \text{silver} \qquad \text{potassium} \qquad \text{ammonia}$$
$$\text{ammoniate} \qquad \text{bromide} \qquad \text{bromide} \qquad \text{nitrate}$$

An emulsion with iodide content may be produced either by direct addition of silver iodide (AgI) before emulsification, or by introducing potassium iodide (KI) during the precipitation process. Silver iodide does not crystallise independently, but (in sufficiently small quantities) forms mixed crystals with silver bromide. The effect of this is to improve sensitivity markedly without any increase in grain size.

The way in which emulsification takes place determines the initial size and size-range of the silver halide grains, which may be modified but not radically changed in later stages of emulsion manufacture. Since grain size distribution is of crucial importance to the ultimate contrast, speed and graininess of an emulsion, the factors which influence it during emulsification are very carefully regulated. These factors include:

(a) the rate of emulsification
(b) the manner of emulsification (intermittent or continuous)
(c) the temperature at which emulsification takes place
(d) the concentration of gelatin
(e) the concentration of the silver nitrate (or ammoniate) solution
(f) the concentration of the alkali bromide solution
(g) the relative proportions of the original solutions
(h) the amount of ammonia (if any) employed and the manner in which it is added.

By regulating the complex chemical interactions which take place between these variables, film stock manufacturers are able to produce emulsions with a wide range of potential characteristics.

Ripening

The emulsion—which still contains at this stage excess alkali halide and by-products of precipitation including alkali nitrate and often ammonia—is next subjected to a heat treatment known as *ripening* (sometimes *first ripening* or *physical ripening*). The emulsion is maintained at a temperature of 40°–80°C. (104°–176°F.) for a time of from ten minutes to two hours, being thoroughly and continually stirred. Now it is found that silver halide crystals are slightly soluble in the excess alkali halide at certain temperatures, and that solubility tends to decrease with increasing grain size. As a result, the smaller crystals pass into solution and re-crystallise out on the larger. This means that as ripening continues, the total number of grains falls, average grain size increases, and the range of grain sizes tends to become wider. The overall growth in size of silver halide grains during a typical ripening process is quite dramatic. The chief factors influencing the extent to which grain sizes change during this stage are:

(a) the time of ripening
(b) the temperature at which ripening takes place
(c) the amount of excess alkali halide
(d) the amount of ammonia (if any)
(e) the amount of iodide (if any)
(f) the concentration of gelatin.

While emulsification affects the potential contrast, speed and graininess of an emulsion, ripening to a very large extent determines its final characteristics. As with emulsification, therefore, the conditions under which the process takes place are subjected to strict regulation.

Chilling, Shredding, Washing

After ripening, the emulsion is chilled into a gel, which prevents further crystallisation, and then shredded into small strips or *noodles* of up to ¼ in.

diameter. Soluble components present during ripening (excess alkali halide, alkali nitrate, ammonia, etc.) are then removed by washing in running water.

This procedure has disadvantages in that certain aspects, in particular the quality of water, are difficult to control. Thus alternatives to the chilling, shredding and washing system have been proposed and are sometimes employed. These include precipitation of the silver halide crystals by coagulation, and extracting the crystals by methods such as centrifuging or sedimentation.

After-ripening

Once the soluble components have been removed, the emulsion shreds are remelted and given a second heat treatment known as *after-ripening* (sometimes called *digestion, second ripening* or *chemical ripening*). During this process the size of the halide grains remains constant but sensitivity is increased by the adsorption of sulphide impurities contained in the gelatin on to the surface of the grains, where they react with the silver halide to form unstable complexes. These complexes gradually decompose to form specks of silver sulphide and metallic silver which, incorporated into the surface structure of the crystals, act as sensitivity centres and greatly speed the reduction of exposed grains when the emulsion is developed.

After-ripening takes place at a temperature of 40°–50°C. (104°–122°F.) for a period of about one hour. The time for different emulsions is critical, since sensitivity cannot rise above a certain level, while fog increases rapidly after a given period. More gelatin, selected for its content of sensitising agents, may be added at this stage. After-ripening may be affected by the presence in the gelatin of certain substances which hinder the formation of sensitivity centres (*antisensitisers*).

The most important influences on the process are thus:
(a) the time of after-ripening
(b) the grain-size distribution established during ripening
(c) the presence of sensitisers
(d) the presence of antisensitisers.

Doctoring

The emulsion is now basically ready for coating, which may take place immediately or after a period of storage. If it is to be stored, organic stabilisers are added, after which it is chilled and shredded again, and then packed in special containers. Maintained at a temperature of 4°–6°C. (39°–43°F.), it will keep for several weeks if necessary. Before coating takes place, however, a number of operations still need to be carried out to modify the physical and chemical characteristics of the emulsion. These operations usually involve the addition of one or more solutions (*doctors*), and doctoring may include:

(a) *Dye sensitisation.* Irrespective of light intensity, silver halides are, without special treatment, sensitive only to ultra-violet, violet and blue light (i.e. in the visible spectrum the range extends to approximately 500nm). By the addition of certain organic dyes (commonly cyanine derivatives) called *spectral sensitisers,* however, this range may be extended to include other regions of the spectrum. *Orthochromatic* film contains dyes which extend the sensitivity range to include green and yellow, i.e. to approximately 600nm. Emulsions containing dyes which extend the range to include the whole of the visible spectrum (or nearly so) are termed *panchromatic,* and most negative emulsions for black-and-white photography are of this type. The spectral sensitivities of typical unsensitised, orthochromatic and panchromatic stocks are compared in Fig. 2.1. Fig. 2.2 illustrates in greater

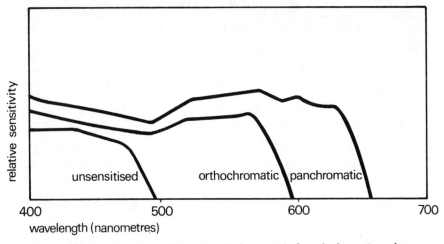

Fig. 2.1. Relative spectral sensitivity of typical unsensitised, orthochromatic and pan-chromatic film stocks

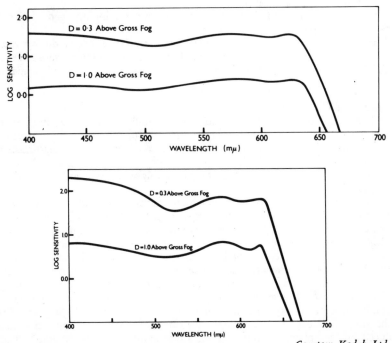

Fig. 2.2. Spectral sensitivity of two commercial motion picture stocks: (above) Eastman Double-X Panchromatic Negative, (below) Eastman 4X Panchromatic Negative

detail the colour sensitivity, at different developed densities, of two black-and-white panchromatic negative films used in professional motion picture photography. The principle of dye sensitisation is widely employed in colour photography, notably in the design of integral tripack film stocks (see Chapter Nine). In addition, cyanine dyes may be used to extend the sensitivity of emulsions into regions beyond the visible spectrum, as in the case of infra-red film.

(b) *Hardening.* Hardening agents such as chrome alum, formalin or chromium acetate are widely used to prevent unnecessary swelling of the emulsion in warm solutions, to decrease the solubility of the emulsion, and to raise its melting point.

(c) *Stabilisation.* Soluble bromides or certain organic compounds may be used as stabilisers. They have the effect of retarding fogging during storage of the completed film, thus improving its keeping properties.

(d) The addition of *wetting agents,* or complex organic substances which reduce the surface tension of the emulsion, thus facilitating the process of coating and reducing the risk of air bubbles forming when the film is wetted by processing solutions.

(e) The addition of alcohol for the purpose of reducing froth formed during coating.

(f) The addition of gold salts and/or polyethylene oxides for increased sensitivity.

(g) The addition of "plasticisers" such as glycerol to improve the flexibility of the dried emulsion layer.

(h) In colour films, the incorporation of colour developing agents or *couplers* (see Chapter Ten.)

Hardening agents and stabilisers may alternatively be added during after-ripening, while it is sometimes preferable to introduce additive substances by the "diffusion" method (i.e. through the protective supercoat) after coating has taken place.

Emulsion Characteristics

The most important characteristics of an emulsion are its contrast, speed and graininess. All of these may be strongly modified by the type of development which the emulsion is given: nevertheless it is perfectly legitimate to speak of a film stock as being "high contrast," "fast," "fine grained" etc., it being understood that these characteristics apply when standard processing is employed.

Contrast describes the way in which an emulsion responds to given variations in exposure. If these variations produce large differences in the blackness or *density* of the developed image, it is said to be a "high contrast" emulsion. High contrast materials have a tendency to exaggerate and compress light and dark tones. If corresponding exposure variations produce relatively small variations in density, the emulsion is said to be "low contrast," and such materials generally have the ability to reproduce faithfully a wide range of greys. *Speed* refers to the sensitivity of the emulsion: with a "high speed" emulsion, a given exposure will affect a comparatively high proportion of the silver halide grains. *Graininess* describes the subjective impression produced by the apparent "clumping" of silver grains in a photographic image when it is enlarged, and is directly proportional to grain size.

During emulsion manufacture, the sensitivity of grains may be increased

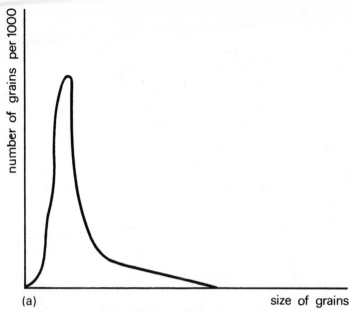

(a)

Fig. 2.3. *Grain-size distribution curves of (a) a high contrast, low speed emulsion (b) a low contrast, high speed emulsion*

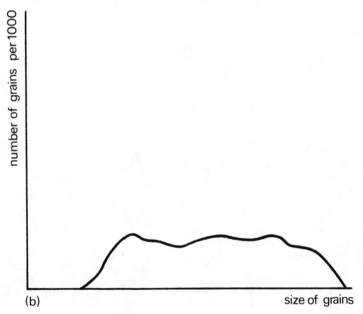

(b)

without altering their size by subjecting them to certain treatments such as the addition of iodide and after-ripening. Once these treatments have been adjusted to produce the optimum benefit, however, it is found that the sensitivity of a grain is directly dependent upon its size: the larger the grain, the more sensitive it is. For this reason, the chief characteristics of an emulsion all depend upon its grain-size distribution (see Fig. 2.3).

Contrast varies according to whether there are small or large differences in the size of grains. If the grains are similar in size, contrast will be high. This is because the sensitivity of all the grains over an area of the emulsion will be roughly the same, and thus above a certain exposure level all the grains will become developable: below it none of them will. A large size-range, on the other hand, will produce low contrast, since the number of developable grains will gradually rise with small increments in exposure.

The speed of an emulsion depends upon the sensitivity, and hence the size, of the more sensitive grains. Graininess, therefore, tends to be directly proportional to speed.

Emulsions are manufactured possessing a wide variety of characteristics, but they may be broadly divided into two classes. The first class consists of high contrast emulsions, which tend also to be slow and fine grained. They

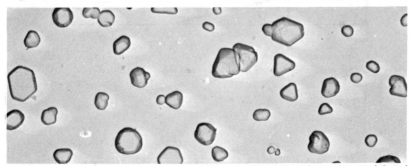

Courtesy Research Laboratories, Kodak Ltd.

Fig. 2.4. Electron micrograph of Eastman XT Negative, a low speed, very fine grain emulsion (x 14,000).

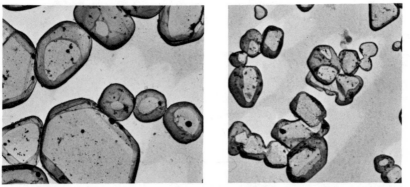

Courtesy Research Laboratories, Kodak Ltd.

Fig. 2.5. Electron micrographs of Eastman 4X Negative, a high speed emulsion: (left) top coat, (right) undercoat (x 14,000).

are produced by restricting the size-range of the halide grains, an effect which is achieved basically by rapid emulsification and a short ripening period. High contrast emulsions are widely used for motion picture positives, variable-area sound recording film and titling stock. The second class consists of high speed emulsions, which tend to be of low contrast and relatively coarse grained. Emulsions of this type have a comparatively large average grain size and a broad grain-size range. In their manufacture, the process of emulsification is drawn out and is often intermittent, while ripening is proportionately long and intense. Most negative materials belong to this class.

B. THE FILM BASE AND COATING OPERATIONS

The Characteristics of the Film Base

The standard base material for motion picture film stock is currently cellulose triacetate, which superseded cellulose nitrate in the years following the Second World War. In contrast to nitrate base, it is non-inflammable and has excellent storage characteristics. Handled and processed with care, it is sufficiently hard, strong, flexible and durable to fulfil the exacting requirements imposed by the necessity of transporting it repeatedly and rapidly by means of mechanical teeth and perforation systems, though it is far from perfect in this respect. It is more dimensionally stable than nitrate base, but still subject to considerable shrinkage. To satisfy optical projection requirements, it is transparent and optically homogeneous, colourless, free from haze (permitting specular transmission) and has a high softening temperature. Chemically, it is stable and inert, being unaffected by processing solutions; it also allows the emulsion a satisfactory key and is resistant to moisture.

Coating

Coating takes place by passing the film base, in broad strips, over a system of rollers by means of which it is brought into contact with the liquid emulsion, etc., to be applied. This may be achieved either by dipping the base directly into a shallow trough containing the liquid, or by passing it next to an intermediate transfer roller.

Sub-coating

The first coating operation involves the application of a sub-stratum or sub-coat (sometimes called a *subbing layer*). This is necessary to provide a suitable key for the gelatin of the emulsion, which would otherwise frill or pucker when wet and strip off when dry. The sub-coat consists of a mixed solution of gelatin and cellulose esters, which on drying becomes a thin layer firmly adhering to the base. It is usual to apply a sub-coat to both sides of the film base, since in this way the tendency of the stock to curl (caused by the uneven shrinkage rates of cellulose triacetate and the emulsion) may be counteracted, and the discharge of static electricity which takes place when the film is rapidly unwound may to some extent be neutralised.

Emulsion Coating

Coating of the doctored emulsion is a critical operation. The thickness and uniformity of the emulsion layer affect the photographic characteristics of the film and are held to rigid specifications, control being exercised by varying the concentration and temperature (and thus the viscosity) of the molten emulsion, and the speed of coating. Control is particularly crucial in the case of films with multilayer emulsions, such as colour stock and some fast negative materials which have a high speed top coat over a slower undercoat.

After coating, the emulsion is set to a gel by chilling, and is then dried and prepared for slitting and chopping to the required size. The manner in which drying takes place is important, since uneven or too rapid drying may affect the speed and other characteristics of the film. All operations involved in emulsion coating normally take place in complete darkness.

Super-coating

The emulsion layer of motion picture film is delicate and subject to surface damage by abrasion and friction. Such damage impairs the quality of the image by rendering the affected halide grains developable, and to counteract it a thin protective layer of gelatin, called a *super-coat* or *non-abrasion layer*, is often applied, particularly to negative. Such a layer may also help to decrease graininess and surface microfogging.

Anti-halation Backings and Dyed Bases

Halation occurs as a result of light which is scattered on striking the emulsion being reflected from the back surface of the film base and re-exposing the film. Such an effect is particularly visible in the case of bright point sources, which become ringed by a second image or halo. *Irradiation*, a related effect, is caused by the scatter of light within the emulsion layer, and results in blurring around the edges of bright areas in the image. Both are illustrated in Fig. 2.6.

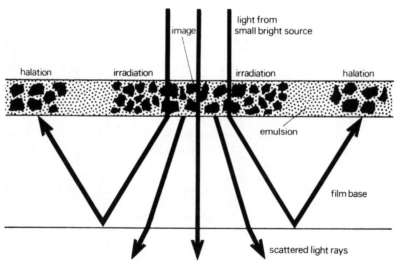

Fig. 2.6. Halation and irradiation

Halation may be minimised by the application of an *anti-halation backing* or by dye treatment of the base. Anti-halation backings contain dyes designed to absorb light of the longest wavelengths to which the emulsion is

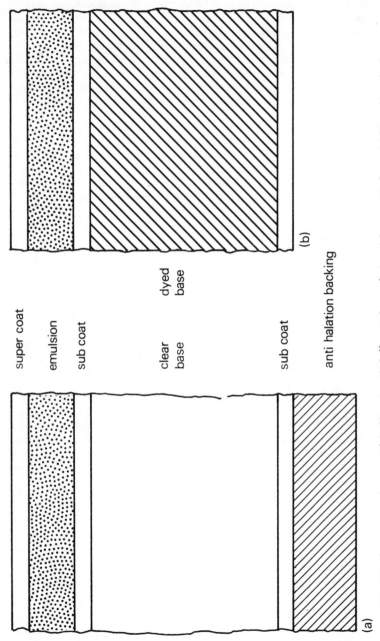

super coat

emulsion

sub coat

clear
base

dyed
base

sub coat

anti halation backing

(b)

(a)

Fig. 2.7. Cross-section (not to scale) through typical film stocks employing (a) an anti-halation backing (b) a dyed base

sensitive, since these rays have the greatest penetrating power. Thus a typical backing for panchromatic film will be blue or grey, to absorb red light. Anti-halation layers are frequently soluble, so that they are easily removed during processing: in this case they are sometimes called "wash-off" backings. Alternatively, halation may be reduced by the use of a film base which is dyed a uniform grey, and which thereby absorbs light travelling in both directions through it. Fig. 2.7 illustrates in cross-section typical film stocks employing (a) an anti-halation backing and (b) a grey base. Irradiation is kept to a minimum by making the emulsion layer or layers as thin as possible.

The Effect of Climatic Conditions on Coated Film Stock

Climatic conditions may affect the storage and keeping properties of coated film stock, particularly prior to processing. The most important factors are:

(a) *Relative humidity.* High relative humidities—above 65-70%—may seriously damage a photographic emulsion by causing mottle, glaze marks and tackiness, decreased sensitivity and increased fog. Such humidities may also invite attack from fungi. At low relative humidities—below about 20%—gelatin tends to become extremely brittle, resulting in sudden emulsion cracks which may extend through to the base.

(b) *Temperature.* At high temperatures acetate film supports have a tendency to become soft and weak and considerable distortion may take place. Moreover, above 21°C. (70°F.) the photographic properties of the emulsion are affected and deterioration may take place within a few hours at temperatures over 100°C. (212°F.). At low temperatures, emulsions tend to become brittle, film speed is lower and contrast and colour balance may also be affected. Provided that the moisture content is maintained, however, filming may be successfully carried out in temperatures as low as —50°C. (—58°F.), assuming that equipment has been appropriately lubricated, etc.

From a practical point of view, however, film must be grossly mishandled before these effects become serious. Even when shooting in extreme tropical conditions, the cameraman can avoid any damage by taking elementary precautions such as sealing all film cans and maintaining them at a relatively even temperature. The greatest danger arises in the case of sudden changes in temperature or humidity, resulting in condensation on the film: refrigeration, therefore, should be used with care. The most critical stage is after exposure and before development, and film should accordingly be processed as soon as possible after shooting.

Chapter III
Processing

The Latent Image

Exposure results in the formation of an invisible latent image, consisting of sub-microscopic specks of metallic silver on the surface of the silver halide grains suspended in the emulsion. (Specks of silver may also form in the interior of halide grains, in which case an *internal latent image* is referred to.) The silver of which these specks are composed is termed *photolytic,* since it is created by the action of light on the silver halide crystals, and tends to be concentrated around the sulphide sensitivity centres (see Chapter Two). When the exposed film is placed in a developing solution, the latent

Fig. 3.1. A Photomec 16mm Processor

Courtesy Bell & Howell Ltd.

image specks act as *development centres,* around which the reduction of the halide to metallic silver takes place. The development centres are believed to be catalytic in operation, acting more and more efficiently the larger they grow: thus the process is auto-accelerated, and in fact during development exposed halide grains are converted to silver 10 to 100 times more rapidly than unexposed grains.

Latent image specks may be extremely minute: some have been detected consisting of no more than two or three silver atoms. However, such specks are too small to act as development centres. Before becoming functional they must reach a critical size, which is not absolute but depends upon the vigour of development. Specks which are too small to trigger reduction under given development conditions constitute what is termed a *sub-latent image.*

The Mechanism of Development

There are two main types of development, "chemical" and "physical." Chemical development, the basic process, acts upon exposed halide grains by reducing them to silver, thus amplifying by an enormous factor the action of light. The reaction may be represented as

$$2AgBr + (d) + H_2O \rightarrow 2Ag + (d)O + 2HBr$$

silver bromide   developer   water   silver   oxidised   hydrobromic
                                              developer   acid

Physical development does not affect the halide of the grain itself, except indirectly. It operates by depositing on the development centres silver which is derived from compounds dissolved in the processing solution. In practice the two operations usually take place in conjunction, chemical development being initially predominant, with physical development playing an increasing role as processing continues. Some degree of physical development is inevitable in any process, because certain essential developer ingredients act to a limited extent as solvents for the silver halide, which after passing into solution is deposited out on the image areas.

Courtesy Filmatic Laboratories

Fig. 3.2. Top view of Photomec machines

Grains are not necessarily reduced in their entirety to metallic silver. A decrease in graininess—at the expense of speed—may be achieved by halting development at a critical point before completion. This is the basis of "fine grain" development.

The colour of the silver constituting a photographic image is explained by the fact that the silver is in close-packed filamentary form. Light striking it is scattered and re-scattered diffusely before being eventually absorbed: thus the silver appears black.

Fog Level

The *fog level* of a developed emulsion refers to that proportion of its density which is unrelated to the image. It comprises:

(a) Grains developed as a result of exposure to gamma rays, cosmic rays, etc. (see Chapter One).

(b) Grains developed as a result of the formation of an unusually large number of highly-active sensitivity specks, which act as development centres without prior exposure. This may happen as a consequence of excessively prolonged after-ripening or poor storage conditions.

(c) Grains developed as a result of the fact that no practical developer can distinguish with 100% accuracy between exposed and unexposed halide crystals. This factor varies widely with the constitution of developing solutions and the conditions—especially time and temperature—of development. Components (a) and (b) develop very rapidly and may be removed without detriment to the image by bleaching immediately after development.

It may be noted that the fog level of a piece of film stock as a whole includes also the density of the triacetate base and of the gelatin of the emulsion.

Developer Ingredients

Developers consist of a finely calculated blend of ingredients, which are classified according to the functions they perform. The four basic constituents are:

(a) the *developing agent* (sometimes called the *reducer* or *reducing agent*)

(b) the *preservative*

(c) the *alkali* (sometimes called the *accelerator* or *activator*)

(d) the *restrainer*.

The Developing Agent

The developing agent performs the basic function of reducing silver halide to metallic silver. Many substances are capable of doing this, but only a few are able to distinguish satisfactorily between exposed and unexposed grains. Developing agents are generally organic compounds, often derivatives of benzene. Common developing agents for motion picture materials include:

(a) *Metol* (monomethyl-paraminophenol sulphate). Marketed under a variety of trade names, Metol gives a comparatively low contrast and high speed (i.e. the critical exposure which makes a grain developable is lower for Metol than for most other developing agents). Operating successfully in a solution of low alkalinity, it produces a high density image valuable for the reproduction of shadow detail, and is also relatively fine grained. Metol is generally employed in conjunction with hydroquinone.

(b) *Phenidone* (1-phenyl-3-pyrazolidone). Phenidone is normally employed, like Metol, as an activator for hydroquinone, since used alone it has a tendency to fog. Its characteristics are also similar to Metol, giving low contrast and high speed, but unlike Metol it is not a benzene derivative.

(c) *Hydroquinone*. A low energy developing agent, hydroquinone requires a strongly alkaline solution. It gives high contrast, though with a tendency to fog fast emulsions. Used in conjunction with Metol ("M.Q." developers) or with Phenidone ("P.Q." developers) it functions as a highly successful agent, more than improving upon the best characteristics of the two components employed separately—a phenomenon called "superadditivity."

(d) *Paraphenylenediamine*. This is the commonest colour developing agent. It is slow-acting and of low energy, with comparatively low speed characteristics. Normally producing fine grained images, it is sometimes combined with Metol to give a higher speed, but with an increase in graininess.

The Preservative

Developing agents have an affinity for oxygen, and if used alone would be quickly oxidised and thus have a very short working life. The first function of the preservative, therefore, is to attract free oxygen, in order to preserve the life of the developing agent. The second function arises from the fact that if unchecked the developing agent would go through various stages of oxidation to form, eventually, insoluble brown final products, causing staining of the image. The preservative must prevent this. Sodium sulphite is found to perform both functions satisfactorily, having an affinity for oxygen, and being able to react with the earlier oxidation products of the developing agent to form comparatively inert colourless compounds.

Sulphite has a solvent effect on silver halide, thus producing a higher rate of physical development. As a result the inclusion of sulphite may increase speed for development to a given contrast. This accelerating action occurs unevenly, being higher in areas of low exposure.

In processes such as colour development, use is made of the oxidation products of the developing agent and for this reason the sulphite content of the solution must be kept low. This increases the risk of uneven activity due to aerial oxidation near the surface of the developing bath, and special precautions need to be taken to counteract this.

The Alkali

The activity of the developer is strongly influenced by the alkalinity of the solution. In fact most developing agents will not work at all without the addition of an alkali, which touches off an acceleration process involving the conversion of some of the original developing agent to its alkali salt. The degree of alkalinity required is determined by the type of developing agent used.

The alkalinity or acidity of a solution is measured on the "pH" scale, which ranges from 0 to 14. 0 represents extreme acidity; 7 is the neutral value, while extreme alkalinity is given by a pH figure of 14. Generally speaking, the higher the pH value, the faster the action of the developing agent, the higher the contrast obtained, and the coarser the grain of the developed image. Thus borax, which creates a pH value of 9, is used with M.Q. or P.Q. developers to produce a low contrast, fine grained result; sodium carbonate (pH 10), again with M.Q. or P.Q. solutions, for a medium grained, higher contrast image; and sodium or potassium hydroxide (pH 12) with hydroquinone developers for highly accelerated, very high contrast results. Other alkalis sometimes employed are sodium sulphite (in the mild range); sodium metaborate and ammonium hydroxide (medium); and paraformaldehyde (strongly alkaline). It is important that accelerators act as buffers, maintaining the alkali level of the solution at a given pH value despite the addition (by means of processing reactions) of further acid or alkali.

Highly active alkalis tend to reduce the working life of the developer and also to stimulate oxidation of the developing agent in solution: for this reason they are often stored apart from the remaining developer ingredients.

Alkalis facilitate development by softening and swelling the emulsion gelatin, allowing easier penetration by the developing agent. Swelling increases with alkalinity, and thus the pH of the solution can also influence the rate of diffusion (see *Agitation and Edge Effects*) and the final density of the image.

The Restrainer

The addition of an alkali to the developing solution results in an accumulation of alkali halide (normally sodium or potassium bromide) as part of the normal process of development. The reaction might thus be given as

$$2HBr + 2NaOH \rightarrow 2NaBr + 2H_2O$$

| hydrobromic acid | sodium hydroxide (alkali) | sodium bromide | water |

In conformity with the Law of Mass Action, development will be retarded by the cumulative build-up of bromide: in fact developer exhaustion normally occurs as a result of this build-up, even though the developing agents have not been completely used up.

During the first stages of development, however, the concentration of alkali bromide is, unless augmented, very low. As a result developing agents have a tendency to operate very vigorously and somewhat indiscriminately, raising fog level by reducing unexposed halide grains, particularly near the surface of the emulsion. The purpose of the restrainer—most commonly potassium bromide—is therefore to retard the action of the developing agent, and because its effect is greatest for unexposed grains and least for exposed grains, the restrainer not only inhibits fogging but also increases the contrast of the image. The soluble bromide may be supplemented by small quantities of other agents known variously as *antifoggants, organic restrainers, fog inhibitors* or *stabilisers*. Substances used for this purpose include benzotriazole and potassium metabisulphite.

The Monitoring of Development

Irrespective of the constituents of the developing solution, the conditions under which development takes place have a crucial effect upon the final results. The emulsion can be made to display desired characteristics only if the following variables are strictly controlled or *monitored:*
(a) the time and temperature of development
(b) agitation of the developing solution
(c) replenishment of the developing solution.

Time and Temperature Control

The longer a film is immersed in developer, the more grains become developed. Thus the effect of increasing development time is to lower the critical exposure at which grains become developable, i.e. film speed rises. So long as fog level remains constant, contrast also increases, since the ratio between the densities of the exposed and unexposed areas of the developed image continues to rise. After a critical point, however, the developer is no longer able to distinguish with any degree of accuracy between exposed and unexposed grains, and fog level rises rapidly. Speed and contrast both reach maximum levels and then slowly drop off. The implications of these relationships for the control of tone rendering are explored more fully in Chapter Five.

Graininess is also affected by the time of development: it tends to increase fairly steadily as development time is prolonged. Thus in processing as in emulsion manufacture it is difficult to achieve an increase in film speed without an equivalent sacrifice in graininess.

The temperature range over which development normally takes place, without pre-hardening of the emulsion, is roughly 13°-24°C. (55°-75°F.). It is limited, at the lower end, by the rate of functioning of developing agents (which in general becomes slower as temperature falls); and at the upper end by the softening of the emulsion gelatin at higher temperatures. Within this range, an increase in temperature of the developing solution is approximately equivalent to an increase of development time, and thus a fall or rise in one of the factors may be compensated for by an appropriate change in the other. This relationship may be illustrated by a time-temperature chart for a given emulsion and contrast (see Fig. 3.3). Altering solution temperature during development is likely to produce many unwanted effects, and thus it is maintained constant by careful control.

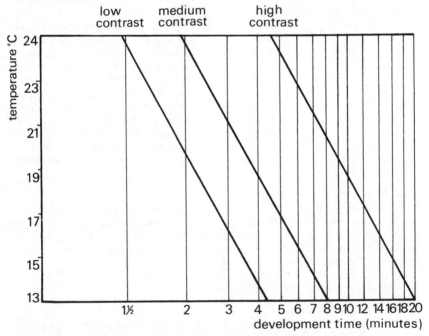

Fig. 3.3. Time-temperature development chart for typical developer and emulsion

The fact that hydroquinone ceases to be effective below a temperature of around 10°C. (50°F.) may be an important consideration in winter. Rinse water will then frequently be below this temperature, thus putting a stop to development immediately the film comes into contact with it, in contrast to the extended development—up to perhaps a minute longer—which occurs during rinsing at other times of the year. If no compensatory measures are taken, film speed will be reduced because of this.

To prevent softening of the gelatin at high temperatures, emulsions specially designed for the purpose may be *pre-hardened*. This technique, used particularly in the case of colour processing, enables the temperature of development to be raised to as high as 43°C. (110°F.), with a consequent saving in time. The quantity of chemicals required for a high-temperature process is also smaller, which means that quick changes can be made if necessary.

Agitation and Edge Effects

If the developing solution is not agitated, a quiescent layer tends to form on the surface of the emulsion, inhibiting the inward diffusion of developing agents and the outward diffusion of development products, thus severely restricting the activity of the developer. Agitation ensures a constant flow of fresh developer to the silver halide crystals. It is worth noting that the rate of development may be increased by agitation only up to a certain point, after which agitation produces little or no change.

Edge or *adjacency effects* are produced by local developer exhaustion, and are greatly intensified by incomplete agitation. Since the emulsion does not receive a constant influx of fresh developer from the solution, the reduction of crystals is affected by the migration of partly-used developer from adjacent areas of the image. In addition, the diffusion of accumulated bromide products tends to retard development in parts of the image lying alongside high density areas. The effect is most evident in the case of a sharp boundary between areas of high and low exposure. The diffusion of partly-exhausted developer and bromide products from the area of high exposure will slow down the rate of development along the edge of the low-exposure area, causing

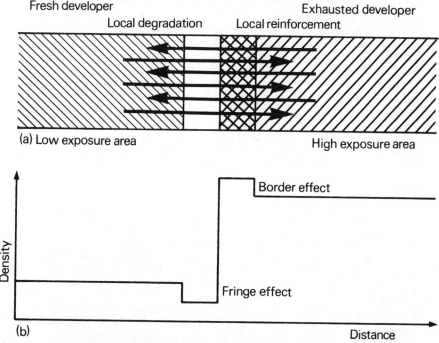

Fig. 3.4. *Simplified representation of edge effects showing (a) local degradation and reinforcement at a sharp image boundary (b) the corresponding density graph*

local degradation. Likewise, the migration of almost fresh developer to the area of high exposure will create a narrow line in which *local reinforcement,* or intensified blackening, occurs. Edge effects are illustrated in Fig. 3.4. Since they result in more abrupt transitions between areas of different densities, and thus improve the sharpness of the image, they are often deliberately cultivated, and "acutance developers" have been designed for this purpose.

Replenishment

The principal changes which occur in the chemical composition of the developing solution as it is used are:

(a) Loss of developing agent due to oxidation

(b) Loss of preservative (sulphite) due to combination with development products to form sulphonates

(c) Decrease in alkalinity due to action of the developer, to a large extent counteracted by increase in alkalinity due to aerial oxidation

(d) Accumulation of by-products, in particular bromide, and also sulphonates, iodide, hydrogen ions etc.

(e) When the developer is the first solution, loss in total volume due to carry-over of the developing solution in the swollen emulsion leaving the developing tank

(f) When the developer is not the first solution, degradation by carry-over from previous baths, e.g. initial rinse or pre-hardening. Of these factors, (d), (e) and (f) are major contributors to developer exhaustion, while (b) and (c) are of minor importance. (a) may be a very significant factor in the case of a high pH developer, particularly if there is a large surface area and good agitation.

To counteract these effects in a continuously operated developing tank a system of *replenishment* must be employed. It is normally insufficient merely to make up the physical volume lost by carry-over of the solution, since the bromide build-up is then too great and exercises a retarding effect. Usually, therefore, replenishment involves also the bleed-off of a certain proportion of the developing solution, and topping up with a special solution containing no bromide. It is found to be uneconomic to attempt to maintain the level of bromide at its initial concentration, since this would require a very high rate of bleed-off; instead bromide concentration is allowed to rise initially, and is then kept steady at a higher level in a state of dynamic equilibrium. Other ingredients are also maintained at a controlled level.

Fixing

After development, the film is normally rinsed in water to remove remaining developer solution and by-products. It then passes into the fixing bath, the purpose of which is to eliminate unexposed silver halide by converting it into soluble complexes, without affecting the silver image. The fixing agents commonly employed are the traditional "hypo" (sodium thiosulphate) and the faster ammonium thiosulphate. Since both of these have a small solvent effect, also, on the silver of the image, fixing times must be carefully limited.

Various acids are generally incorporated in the fixing solution to prevent, by neutralisation, any further development resulting from the action of residual developing solution on the film. This is crucial, since in the presence of the fixing solution any action of the developer causes fogging; in addition, staining may result from oxidation of the developer when the preservative has been diluted. A sulphite is also incorporated to preserve the fixer from decomposition by acid.

A further ingredient of the fixing solution is an agent such as white alum or chrome alum. This hardens the emulsion, which tends to become swollen and softened by passing through the processing baths.

Washing and Drying

The film is then given a final wash, which for motion picture materials must fulfil stringent requirements. This is because any residual silver salts will soon decompose to form brown stains, while thiosulphate will slowly attack the silver image, and may also cause discoloration. Washing efficiency increases as the temperature of the water is raised, but a maximum of 24°C. (75°F.) is set by the danger of softening of the gelatin, if it has not been pre-hardened.

The final stage is drying. The film is placed in circulating warm air until the swollen emulsion layer is dehydrated to its normal dry state. A residual moisture content of 10-15% must be maintained to prevent the gelatin from becoming brittle and cracking. The air used for drying must not be too hot (in which case shrinkage results) nor too humid (which may cause an increase in the density of the silver image as a result of the settling of silver crystals in the gelatin binder). Even after correct drying, the emulsion layer remains soft for some time, and "green" film direct from processing should not be projected if scratches are to be avoided. If possible, the film should be lubricated by waxing.

Silver Bleaches

Some photographic procedures, including reversal processing and colour processing, require the developed silver image to be removed by *bleaching*. In simple bleaches, the silver is converted into soluble silver complexes, while *rehalogenising bleaches* (used in colour processing) re-convert the silver image to insoluble silver halide. Bleaches may also be combined with a fixing solution which simultaneously removes residual silver halide.

Reversal Processing

Reversal processing is an alternative to the basic negative/positive photographic system. After regular development producing a negative image, processing is continued to reverse tonalities for a second time. Thus, for example, a positive transparency may be created directly from the original camera film. The basic stages of the process are:

(a) *First development.* This is as the usual negative/positive process, except that a silver halide solvent such as sodium thiocyanate, ammonia or sodium thiosulphate may be added in order to reduce the density of the potential image, thus helping to produce clear highlights.

(b) *Bleaching.* The silver constituting the negative image is removed by a bleaching solution such as potassium dichromate or an acid permanganate.

(c) *Second exposure.* The film is then uniformly exposed to light, rendering the remaining silver halide developable. This step may be omitted if a fogging agent is incorporated in the second developing solution.

(d) *Second development.* The residual silver halide is converted to metallic silver, forming a positive image.

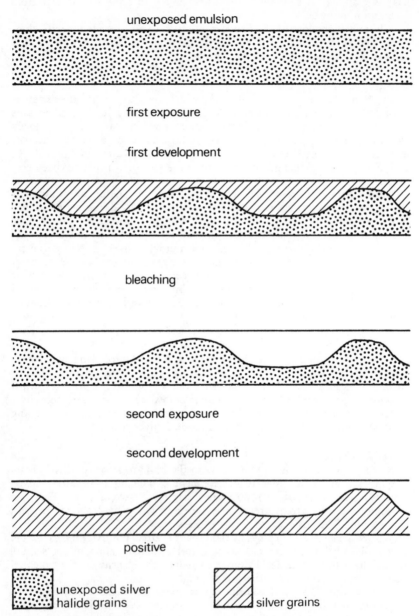

unexposed emulsion

first exposure

first development

bleaching

second exposure

second development

positive

unexposed silver halide grains

silver grains

Fig. 3.5. Reversal processing

These stages are illustrated in Fig. 3.5. Other procedures involved may include intermediate rinse and stop baths; immersion in sodium sulphite solution following bleaching to re-sensitise the emulsion; and a final fixing-hardening bath to remove the residuum of silver halide which has escaped attention from both developers.

Exposure latitude is very much more critical with reversal than with negative/positive films (see Chapter Five).

Solarisation is a partial reversal effect caused by rehalogenation of silver grains. This is generally brought about when the emulsion gelatin, which normally acts as a halogen acceptor, has become saturated. Excess bromine then tends to recombine with latent image specks (assuming it is dark), forming a protective coat on the exposed grains and preventing them from becoming developed. Solarisation, properly so called, occurs on rare occasions as the result of extreme over-exposure, such as in the photography of lightning; the term is commonly applied, however, to another form of reversal which occurs following re-exposure after development has been partially completed. The latter is more correctly called the "Sabattier effect" and may be deliberately induced and controlled in the laboratory.

Chapter IV
Sensitometry

Sensitometry is the study of the response of photographic emulsions to light, under varied processing conditions. The method employed is to subject an emulsion to a wide range of carefully controlled exposures, process it according to desired specifications, and then to measure accurately the range of resulting densities. By plotting measured densities on a graph against exposure values, a series of *characteristic curves* for an emulsion given various times, etc., of development may be arrived at, and from these, measurements of the contrast, speed, fog level and other characteristics of the film may be derived.

The Sensitometer

The instrument used for giving a known and strictly regulated series of exposures to a strip of test film is known as a *sensitometer*. Sensitometers may be either *intensity-scale* or *time-scale* devices: in the first, the emulsion is given a series of exposures graduated according to light intensity, while in the second exposures are varied according to time. Because of Reciprocity Law Failure (see Chapter One) and the fact that especially in cinematography the important differences in exposure values arise from differences in subject luminance rather than length of exposure, intensity-scale devices are preferable.

Exposures varying in intensity could be given by raising and lowering the output of the test lamp. However the colour temperature of a tungsten light source varies with the voltage which is fed to it, and since no emulsion is uniformly sensitive to all regions of the visible spectrum, this method would result in undesirable variations in emulsion response. The technique therefore employed is to use a lamp or lamps emitting light of a given intensity which is varied in its effect on the film by being transmitted through a graduated *optical wedge,* or filter, with continuous or, more usually, stepped increases in density (Fig. 4.1). The colour temperature of the light source

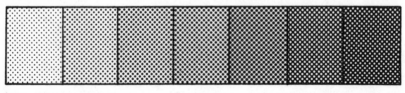

top

side

Fig. 4.1. Optical step wedge (section)

is accurately controlled to reproduce the conditions either of standard daylight or of standard tungsten lighting, while the optical wedge—usually consisting of a dispersion of carbon in gelatin—must be of neutral density, i.e. have no effect on the colour composition of the source.

The scale chosen for the steps in the optical wedge is geometric. This corresponds approximately with the way in which the eye perceives tonal differences: if the luminance of a subject is doubled and then doubled again, for example, the tone luminance changes will appear constant. In a typical optical wedge there are 21 steps, each increasing in density so that on every second step the exposure is halved, and the total exposure range is approximately 1000:1. Since the maximum luminance range of a sunlit subject very seldom exceeds 500:1, and this range is reduced in the camera due to interior reflections and light scatter (*lens* and *camera flare*), the standard sensitometric range of exposures amply exceeds the range likely to be encountered in normal photographic work.

Fig. 4.2. Kodak Type 6 High Intensity Sensitometer; (below) exploded view

In practice it is impossible to manufacture step wedges with absolutely precise increments in density. Each wedge is therefore individually calibrated with respect to its departures from the norm, and appropriate allowances are made when measuring emulsion response.

In a typical intensity-scale sensitometer, the lamp is mounted on a carriage which is enclosed except for a slit aperture at the base. The carriage is moved at a constant speed over the optical wedge, which is placed in contact with the emulsion.

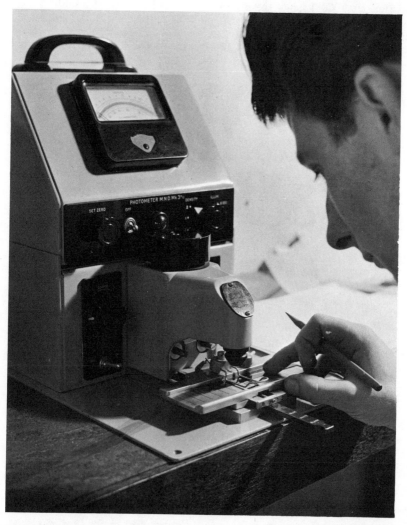

Fig. 4.3. Baldwin densitometer

Courtesy Filmatic Laboratories

The Densitometer

A *densitometer* is an instrument for measuring the light-stopping capacity of a developed photographic image. A *transmission densitometer* is used for transparent film, and is thus the basic instrument for motion picture purposes. Transmission densitometers formerly employed the principle of visual comparison with a test surface, but this type has now been almost universally superseded by devices incorporating a photo-electric cell or electronic phototube. Densitometers of modern design consist essentially of:

(a) a lamp and optical system to direct a fixed beam of light on to, and through, the section of film to be tested

(b) a light-sensitive receptor to measure the proportion of incident light transmitted by the film

(c) an indicating circuit incorporating an amplifier and an indicating meter (see Fig(see Fig. 4.4).

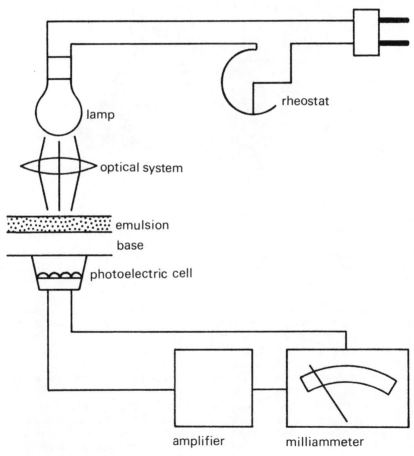

Fig. 4.4. Photo-electric densitometer: basic layout

A rheostat is sometimes incorporated in the lamp circuit so that the intensity of the light source may be adjusted. Heat-absorbing and dichroic filters in the light path are necessary to eliminate unwanted infra-red response. The indicating meter is normally calibrated from 0 to 3.0 or 4.0 in units of *Density* (see next section). On some instruments, such as that illustrated in Fig. 4.5, the meter dial is replaced by a digital display panel.

Fig. 4.5. Macbeth TD 404 Densitometer   *Courtesy Macbeth Instrument Corp.*

Transmission of light through a parallel-sided medium may, like reflection from a surface, be specular or diffuse. Transmission through a photographic film is essentially specular, but a certain proportion of incident light, depending upon the graininess, contrast and density of the image, may be scattered by the emulsion and transmitted diffusely. A reading of *diffuse density* is obtained from a densitometer when illumination is perpendicular to the emulsion and *all* the transmitted light is measured, or alternatively when illumination of the emulsion is diffuse (by the use, for example, of opal glass) and only specularly transmitted light is measured. *Specular density* is gauged by illuminating the emulsion directly and measuring only the specular proportion of the transmitted light. The methods are illustrated in Fig. 4.6. A measurement of *double diffuse density* may also be made. The distinction is significant because either specular or diffuse light may be used in printing (see Chapter Seven). Many densitometers may be adjusted for either diffuse or specular density measurements, though diffuse readings are more common.

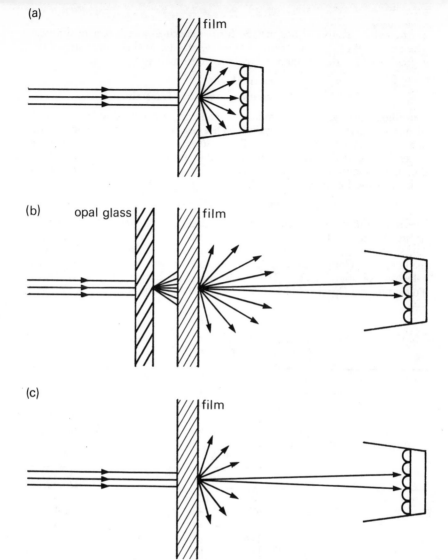

Fig. 4.6. Methods of measuring (a) diffuse density using specular illumination (b) diffuse density using diffuse illumination (c) specular density

Transmittance, Opacity, Density

The units used for the measurement of emulsion light-stopping ability are of considerable importance. *Transmittance,* or the *Transmission Factor,* is defined simply as the proportion of incident light which is transmitted, expressed as a fraction or percentage:

$$\text{Transmittance} = \frac{\text{Transmitted Light}}{\text{Incident Light}}$$

49

(If necessary, Transmittance may be further specified as specular or diffuse.) The reciprocal of this ratio, termed *Opacity,* may be used as a measure of the degree to which the medium prevents light from passing:

$$\text{Opacity} = \frac{\text{Incident Light}}{\text{Transmitted Light}} = \frac{1}{\text{Transmittance}}$$

Sensitometric measurements could be made in terms of Opacity, but disadvantages accrue from the way in which Opacity rises at an ever increasing rate with diminishing values of Transmittance. In addition, photographic materials essentially have a geometric, rather than arithmetic response. It is thus more convenient and appropriate to use a logarithmic unit. *Density* is defined as the logarithm (to the base 10) of Opacity:

$$\text{Density} = \text{Log}_{10}\text{Opacity}$$

The minimum value of Density is 0, corresponding to 100% Transmittance or an Opacity of 1; while the maximum value of Density seldom exceeds 3.0, since an emulsion which transmits only 0.1% of incident light is virtually opaque ($\log_{10}1000 = 3.0$). Satisfactory negatives in fact rarely exceed a Density of approximately 2.6. The relationships between typical values of Transmittance, Opacity and Density are given in Table 4.1.

TABLE 4.1

Relationships between Selected Values of Transmittance, Opacity and Density

A	B	C		D	E
Incident Light (candelas)	Transmitted Light (candelas)	Transmittance or Transmission Factor (B/A)		Opacity (A/B)	Density (Log Opacity)
		%			
100	100	1	100	1	0
100	80	4/5	80	1.25	0.09
100	50	1/2	50	2	0.3
100	20	1/5	20	5	0.7
100	10	1/10	10	10	1.0
100	5	1/20	5	20	1.3
100	1	1/100	1	100	2.0
100	0.1	1/1000	0.1	1000	3.0

The Characteristic Curve

In order to express graphically the characteristics of a film, as derived from a set of sensitometric figures, it is next necessary to plot figures of Density against their corresponding Exposure values. Exposure could be plotted directly, in units, for example, of foot-candela-seconds, but since the exposures given by a sensitometer increase in geometric steps it is preferable to use a logarithmic scale on this axis, as well. If, therefore, figures of Density (D), on a vertical axis, are plotted against figures of Log_{10}Exposure (log E) on a horizontal axis, a curve of the type shown in Fig. 4.7 may be derived from typical sensitometric data. This is known as the *characteristic curve* of an emulsion, often shortened to *characteristic* and sometimes known as the "D log E" curve (from the respective axes) or the "H & D" curve (after pioneer photographic researchers Hurter and Driffield).

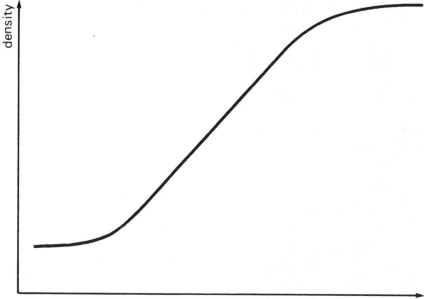

Fig. 4.7. *Characteristic curve*

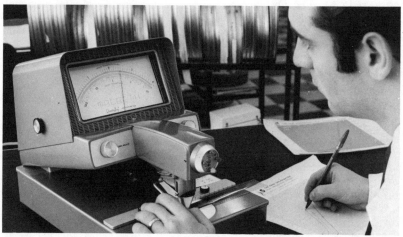

Fig. 4.8. *Plotting characteristic curves with the aid of a densitometer*

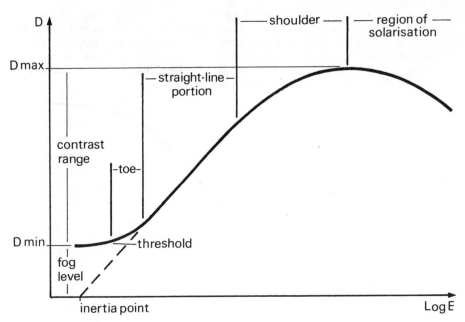

Fig. 4.9. Features of the characteristic curve

The Properties of the Characteristic Curve

The general profile of a characteristic curve (see Fig. 4.9) is as follows:

(a) a horizontal section at fog level, in which increases in log E do not produce measurable increases in D

(b) a curved portion, known as the *toe* of the characteristic, in which the emulsion begins to react at an ever increasing rate to increases in log E

(c) a straight-line portion, in which increases in D are directly proportional to increases in log E

(d) a gently curved section, known as the *shoulder,* in which increases in log E produce progressively smaller increases in D

(e) a downward-curved portion, the region of reversal or solarisation, in which further increases in log E produce decreases in D.

The *minimum density* or fog level of a film is determined by the density of the base and the fog level of the emulsion, in combination. The point on the characteristic curve at which an increase in log E first results in a measurable increase in D is known as the *threshold,* while another measure of the initial reaction of the emulsion, the *inertia point,* is established by extending the straight-line portion to meet the log E axis. Beyond the threshold, on the toe of the characteristic, exposures do produce levels of density distinct from fog level, but in this region the response of the emulsion is distorted. Since increases in exposure do not produce proportionate increases in density, dark tones are compressed and shadow detail may be lost. Provided that shadow detail is not lost, however—i.e. assuming that the gradient of the curve is sufficient to differentiate between small increments in log E—exposures on the toe of the characteristic are acceptable and in some cases may be compensated for in printing.

The straight-line portion represents that range in which exposure values will produce a "correct" negative, in which tonal differences of the original subject are associated with proportional differences in density, without contrast distortion and without the need for printing compensation. The values of log E covered by the straight-line portion of the characteristic were originally thought to constitute the only acceptable exposure range, but modern theory has considerably modified this view.

The *useful exposure range* of an emulsion may be defined as that range of exposure values lying between the minimum and maximum acceptable exposure levels. The minimum value, corresponding with the speed point in current speed rating systems (see below) requires a certain density above fog level in combination with a sufficiently high curve gradient. Maximum useful exposure is limited by the increase in graininess, with corresponding loss in resolving power, resulting from high exposure levels. The critical point may in fact lie below the shoulder of the characteristic.

Exposures on the shoulder of the curve again produce distorted density values. This is the range of over-exposure, in which the highlights of a scene are burnt out. Beyond the point of *maximum density,* severe over-exposure results in solarisation (see Chapter Three) with corresponding decreases in image density. The *contrast range* is the total range of densities, from minimum to maximum, of which the film is capable.

Analysis of film response by this method is complicated by the fact that the characteristics of many modern fast emulsions have no, or at the very most a very short straight-line portion. In these, it tends to become supplanted by a point of inflexion serving to separate an extended toe region from an extended shoulder region (see Fig. 4.10). Nevertheless, with suitable modification most of the above observations remain valid, though it is obvious that no range of log E increments will produce exactly proportionate density

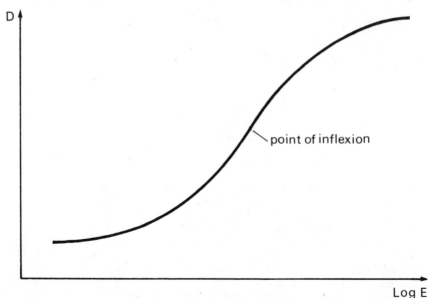

Fig. 4.10. Characteristic curve of a modern fast emulsion, having no straight-line portion

changes, while the areas of "under-exposure" and "over-exposure" can in no way be defined merely by reference to their position with respect to the straight-line portion of the characteristic.

Emulsion characteristics are, of course, dependent upon the processing which the film is given. When no mention of processing is made, it is assumed that the film is to be developed to a standard specification, often recommended by the manufacturer.

The Measurement of Gamma

Among the most significant features of a film characteristic is the slope, or gradient, of its straight-line portion. Consider the reproduction of a given range of log E values by (a) an emulsion with a steeply sloped characteristic, and (b) an emulsion with a gently sloped characteristic (Fig. 4.11).

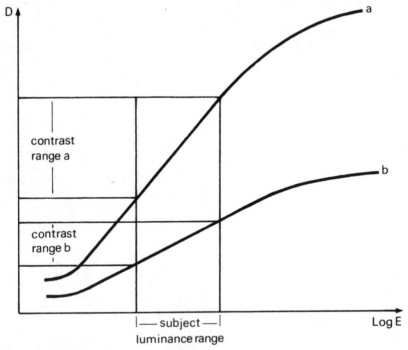

Fig. 4.11. *Reproduction of a subject with given luminance range by emulsions having characteristics of different gradients*

It is evident that emulsion (a) produces larger variations in density for given exposure increments than emulsion (b). Now this relationship can reveal much about the potential contrast of the developed film. If we consider the given range of log E values as the luminance range of the subject being photographed, it may be seen that emulsion (a) will produce a high contrast negative, while emulsion (b), with the same subject, will have comparatively low contrast results. The slope of the straight-line portion of a characteristic is thus a measure of the *potential contrast* (sometimes called *contrastiness*) of an emulsion-development combination.

Gamma (γ) is the term employed to describe the slope of the character-istic, and is defined as the tangent of the angle (x) formed when the straight-line portion is extended to meet the horizontal axis (see Fig. 4.12).

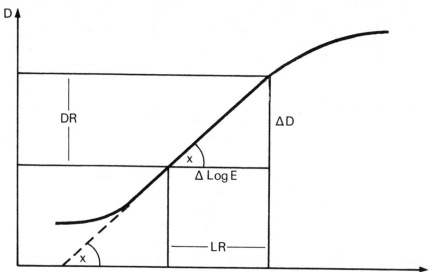

Fig. 4.12. Measurement of gamma   Log E

This is equal to an increase in density ($\triangle$D) divided by its equivalent log E increase ($\triangle$log E) for any range of log E values lying below the straight-line portion, a ratio which may also be expressed in terms of density range (DR) and its corresponding luminance range (LR):

$$\gamma = \tan \angle x = \frac{\triangle D}{\triangle \log E} = \frac{DR}{LR}$$

Gamma thus indicates the ratio by which subject luminance levels will be either expanded or compressed in the photographic image. High gamma values are equivalent to high potential contrast, and vice versa.

While exposure increments will be reproduced *proportionately* if they fall within the area covered by the straight-line portion of the characteristic, no matter what its slope, there is only one value of gamma at which density increments will be *equal* to their corresponding variations in subject lum-inance. This is the gamma value of 1, where the slope of the straight-line portion is 45°. It is generally the object in motion picture production to achieve approximately unity gamma in the final projection print as it is viewed by a theatrical audience (see Chapter Seven).

For characteristics without a straight-line section, it is necessary to arrive at an *average gradient* figure. This may be done by a variety of methods depending upon the purpose for which the emulsion is designed. Techniques include measuring between fixed density or fixed log exposure values; using a specified density and log exposure increment; and calculating a *point gradient*, i.e. the slope of the tangent to the curve at a specified point. It may be noted that the slope at the point of inflexion will give the highest point gradient value for any normal curve.

In Chapter Two it was stated that high contrast emulsions have a tendency to exaggerate and compress light and dark tones. This may be explained in terms of sensitometric analysis by the fact that useful exposure range normally decreases with higher gamma values. Thus there is a greater likelihood of exposure values lying outside the straight-line portion, on the shoulder and toe of the characteristic, and hence of highlights and shadows of the original subject being distorted.

Gamma is a measure of the *potential* contrast which an emulsion with a certain type of development is capable of producing. The actual contrast of a developed photographic image, usually measured by the *contrast ratio,* is dependent also upon the subject luminance range of the original (together with the flare factor) and upon whether or not the exposure is made entirely on the straight-line portion of the characteristic. Thus a photograph of a high contrast subject developed to a low gamma may have the same final contrast as a photograph of a subject with a narrow luminance range developed to a high gamma (see Fig. 4.13).

Contrast ratio is defined as the ratio between maximum and minimum Opacities (O) of the photographic image, i.e.

$$\text{Contrast ratio} = \frac{\text{Omax}}{\text{Omin}}$$
$$= \text{antilog (Dmax—Dmin)}.$$

For example, if maximum Density is 2.3 and minimum Density 0.8, the contrast ratio is the antilog of 1.5, or 32:1.

Speed Rating Systems

The position of a characteristic curve on the graph relative to the log E axis determines, in a general way, the speed of the emulsion. The problems of developing a system for quoting film speed in numerical terms are, however, complicated by the fact that characteristics differ in shape as well as position. A number of alternative methods have been employed in the past, illustrating different approaches:

(a) *H & D.* Hurter and Driffield extended the straight-line portion of the curve to meet the log E axis and used this point—which is in fact the inertia point—as a reference. Because many modern emulsions have very long toe regions on which exposures may usefully be made, the H & D system has been superseded.

(b) *Scheiner.* The original Scheiner system used the threshold, or point at which an image density is just perceptible. The method suffered from two basic disadvantages: firstly that the point was difficult to locate with precision, and secondly that an indefinite portion of the curve above the threshold was not usable for photographic purposes because contrast was still too low.

(c) *Old DIN.* The original German standard was based on the exposure required to achieve a density of 0.1 above fog level.

(d) *Minimum Useful Gradient.* This system, recognising the importance of contrast as well as density in determining speed, specified 0.2 as the minimum useful gradient of an emulsion, and used the exposure value at which this gamma was reached as a point of reference.

(e) *Old ASA/BSI.* Minimum useful gradient gives a distorted impression by being fixed arbitrarily, however, since it is a function of emulsion gamma.

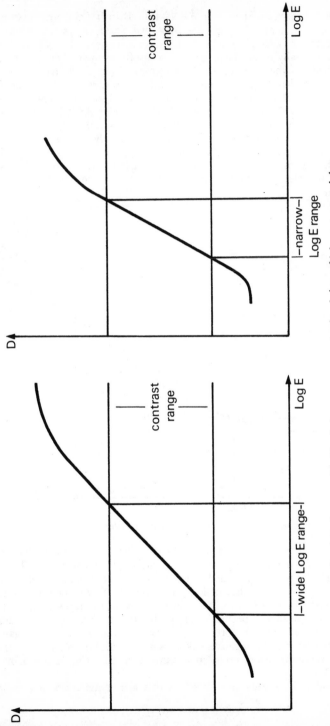

Fig. 4.13. *Images with identical contrast range produced from high contrast and low contrast subjects by the use of emulsions developed to low and high gamma values respectively*

The original American Standards Association/British Standards Institution method refined system (d) into the *fractional gradient* system, which entailed making an average gradient measurement over the region where exposure was ideally to be made, minimum useful gradient being defined as a fixed fraction of the effective emulsion gamma figure so derived.

These systems have become generally replaced as a result of the adoption by the United States, Britain and Germany in 1960–62 of a new standard: (f) *New ASA/BSI/DIN.* The drawback of the older ASA/BSI system was that although it produced satisfactory results it was rather complicated and cumbersome. Measurements could be made more easily, it was decided, if it was stipulated that all films to be tested be developed to a single specified gamma. The exposure required to produce a fixed density above fog level could then be selected with confidence as the point from which to derive a speed rating.

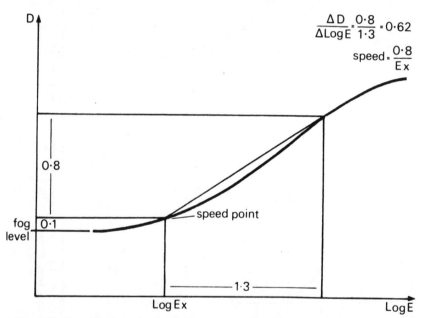

Fig. 4.14. Determination of speed in the current ASA system

The new system is illustrated in Fig. 4.14. The *speed point* is defined as that exposure E_x required to produce a density of 0.1 above fog level (as in the older DIN system) provided that the film is developed to an average gradient of 0.62 over the range of log E between log E_x and (log E_x + 1.3), i.e. over a range of exposures varying in intensity in the ratio of 20:1. (Although the system is not specifically applicable to cine films, it may be noted that this stipulated gradient corresponds closely to the recommended gamma for most motion picture negative stocks, which is 0.65.) Now if E_x is expressed in metre-candela-seconds, an arithmetic speed rating is given by the formula $0.8/E_x$.

ASA (and BSI) speeds are quoted in this arithmetic form: a film with an ASA speed of 400 is thus twice as fast, and requires half the exposure of one with an ASA speed of 200. The German standard, DIN, uses a geometric scale in which doubling the speed is indicated by a numerical increase of 3: thus a DIN speed of 27 (equivalent to 400 ASA) indicates that a film is twice as fast as one with a speed of 24 (200 ASA).

The purpose of a speed rating system is to facilitate correct exposure for a given film stock. In the old ASA/BSI system, a substantial margin for error in exposure calculation, and for the accommodation of subjects with an exceptionally wide luminance range, was allowed for by incorporating a safety factor of 2.35, or 0.37 log E units. With growing acceptance that exposures on the toe of the characteristic could produce satisfactory results, the new system reduced this constant to a factor of 1.2, or 0.08 log E units. Current ASA speed ratings are thus approximately twice the old ones.

It is important to note that some prominent motion picture film stock manufacturers have not changed to the new ASA system, continuing to quote "Exposure Index" figures equivalent to the old rating and incorporating the safety factor as before. Occasionally both speeds are quoted by the manufacturer, as "minimum" (new) and "average" (old) exposure meter settings. Speed ratings depend also upon the colour temperature of the light source employed, and manufacturers normally quote separate speeds for daylight and tungsten use, the former (in the case of black-and-white stocks) being usually the higher.

Exposure recommendations may alternatively be incorporated in an *incident light table* for a given emulsion, which gives direct information as to the number of foot-candles necessary, assuming an average subject, at a range of different f/stops, as for example:

ILLUMINATION (INCIDENT LIGHT) TABLE FOR TUNGSTEN LIGHT

Shutter speed approximately $\frac{1}{50}$ second—24 frames per second

Lens apertures	f/1.4	f/2.0	f/2.8	f/4.0	f/5.6	f/8.0
No. of foot-candles required	10	20	40	80	160	320

The current ASA/BSI/DIN system is applicable only to those materials which can realistically be developed to a control gamma of 0.62, that is most negative stocks for original camera use. Exposure recommendations for other types of film, for example high contrast stock for titling, may be given in the form of an incident light table or in a more specialised fashion according to the purpose for which the stock is designed.

Quoted speeds give a very accurate indication of the potential performance of a particular sample of film stock. While it is true that film of a given ASA rating may vary in speed from batch to batch, such variations are in practice extremely small, since the manufacturers work within very close tolerances. If a cameraman finds he is consistently under- or over-exposing film while working at the rated speed, it is much more likely to be the result of inaccurate calibration of his light meter or irregularity in his method of taking readings with it, than a departure in the actual sensitivity of the film stock from its quoted speed rating.

Chapter V
Image Formation and Tone Rendering

Sensitometry provides the analytical tools with which the response of emulsions under varied conditions of exposure and development may be studied. This chapter is concerned with the application of these tools in order to discover the optimum conditions for high-quality photographic results. The most important matter for investigation is the theory of tone reproduction, or the manner in which gradations in luminance in the original subject are converted into density increments in the photographic image. As with previous chapters, the analysis refers primarily to black-and-white materials, though the principles remain basically the same for colour.

Types of Camera Negative Film Stock

Motion picture negative stocks for original shooting purposes are generally designed to be developed to a fixed gamma, 0.65, no matter what their speed. The reasons for this are given later in the chapter. Thus the chief feature which distinguishes a typical fast negative stock from a slower film (apart from its greater graininess) is the fact that it requires less light to produce a given density, i.e. its characteristic curve lies further to the left (see Fig. 5.1). In addition, a faster stock has a slightly higher fog level and, being more sensitive, dates more rapidly than a slower film. It is not possible to generalise about the contrast range or useful exposure range of fast as compared with slow stocks, since these characteristics are to a great extent dependent upon the peculiarities of specific emulsions.

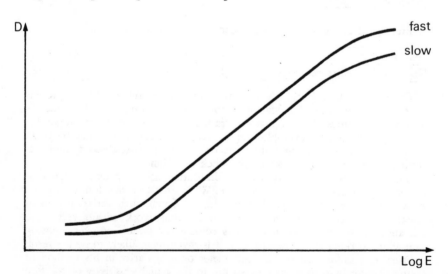

Fig. 5.1. Comparative characteristics of typical fast and slow camera negative stocks, when developed to the same gamma.

Apart from general purpose camera negative materials, film stocks are manufactured with specific characteristics for a number of special types of filming. These include low-speed fine-grain negative stocks from which positives for back-projection may be taken; high-speed negatives for slow-motion cinematography; and telerecording stock for filming directly from a television screen. Special requirements determine the characteristics of *titling stock,* which is used for filming black-and-white titles, etc., when it is desirable that no intermediate grey tones should be recorded. In this case, the object of exposure control is to ensure that all the luminance levels of the subject lie *outside* the "useful exposure range" of the emulsion. Titling stock (see Fig. 5.2) therefore has a very steep gradient, with a recommended gamma of from 3.6 to 4.0, which generally results in an image sharply divided, as desired, into areas of jet black and clear transparency. Since illumination conditions are under complete control, titling stock is normally slow and blue-sensitive only.

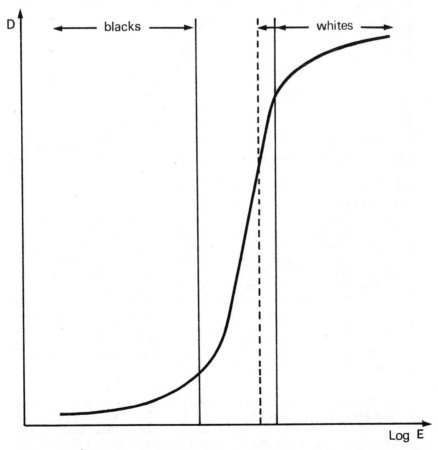

Fig. 5.2. *Characteristic of a typical titling film stock, showing regions of the curve used in exposure control. Dotted line indicates portion of the straight line which may be used in practice to prevent danger of irradiation and halation caused by over-exposure of whites.*

Reversal Film Stock

The requirements of reversal processing mean that, compared with the equivalent negative film, reversal stocks (see Fig. 5.3) are more contrasty, slightly slower and have a smaller useful exposure range. They also have a finer grain structure (see Chapter Six) and tend to have a slightly lower fog level.

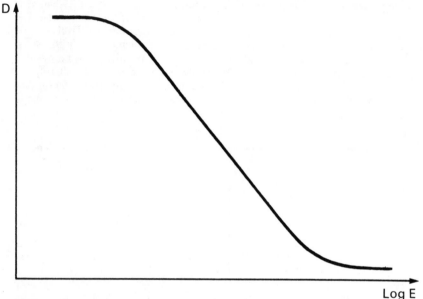

D

Log E

Fig. 5.3. Characteristic of a typical reversal film stock

Subject Luminance Range

The range of luminance values in the scene to be photographed is known as the *subject luminance range*. Focussed into an image on the emulsion, these areas of different luminance will produce different log exposure values. The normal object of photographic exposure control is to so render these differing luminances that they produce equivalent tonal variations in the final print, and for this purpose the variations must be rendered proportionately in the negative. The *total* luminance range of a subject is seldom reproduced exactly on film: this is because of flare (see below) and other practical limitations of the photographic process. The luminance range of the subject is therefore rendered by a *compressed* range of negative densities, but provided proportionate tonal relationships are maintained satisfactory photographic quality results.

Flare

Lens flare is caused by light which is reflected from glass/air interfaces of the lens components reaching the emulsion. It may be greatly reduced, though not entirely eradicated, by the coating of lens surfaces. Dust, scratches, etc. on the lens increase the risk of flare. *Camera flare* results from stray reflections from the lens barrel, the shutter, the iris diaphragm, interior camera surfaces etc.

Flare illumination is normally spread fairly uniformly over the film surface. But in a case where part of the subject is exceptionally bright, a "ghost image" of it may be formed. Alternatively, an unfocussed image of the diaphragm, sometimes termed a "flare spot," may be produced.

The *flare factor* may be defined as the ratio of subject luminance range, Lr, to image illumination range, Ir:

$$\text{Flare factor} = \frac{\text{Lr}}{\text{Ir}} = \frac{\text{Lmax}-\text{Lmin}}{\text{Imax}-\text{Imin}}$$

The effect of flare may be illustrated by a flare curve drawn on a graph with log image illumination (log I) on the vertical axis and log subject luminance (log L) on the horizontal axis (see Fig. 5.4). The 45° line represents equality between subject luminance and image illumination levels, or a flare factor of 1. It is evident that maximum deviation of the flare curve from the 45° line occurs at lower levels of subject luminance. Flare, that is, being scattered in a random manner over the emulsion, has a greater effect on shadow areas than on the highlights of an image. For example, the addi-

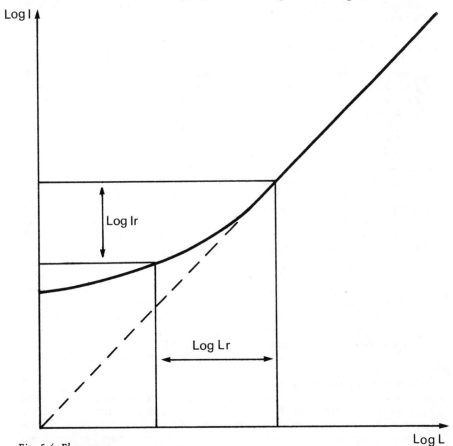

Fig. 5.4. Flare curve

tion of 2 flare units to a subject having a ratio between maximum and minimum luminances of 100:1 increases the illumination of the highlight area by 2%, but that of the deepest shadow by 200%.

Even a small flare component may have a very great influence on the luminance ratio of the subject as it is converted into an image in the camera. Fortunately, this compression effect is not constant for all ranges of illumination, but is highest for high contrast subjects (which would, in any case, be beyond the limitations of the film stock) and lowest for those subjects in which the contrast ratio is already low. The effect of flare on subject luminance ratio is shown in simplified form in the following table, which assumes a constant maximum illumination:

Subject luminance ratio	1000:1	500:1	100:1	50:1	10:1	5:1
Flare (%)	2	2	2	2	2	2
Image illumination ratio	50:1	50:1	34:1	25:1	8:1	4.6:1

In colour photography, flare results in desaturation, since flare illumination consists of a mixture of light from all parts of the subject and is therefore usually white, or very close to white.

Exposure Latitude

The next topic for consideration is the positioning of the subject, whose range of luminances has been compressed by the flare factor, on the characteristic curve. For this purpose it is convenient to assume a flare factor of 1, so that the subject luminance range is identical to the camera image illumination range.

The normal object of exposure control is clearly to ensure that the tones of the original subject are reproduced without distortion and without loss of detail. The concept of the "useful exposure range" of an emulsion was introduced in the previous chapter to cover precisely those values of log E which produce acceptable photographic results. The object may thus be restated as that of ensuring that the subject luminance range falls somewhere within the useful exposure range of the film.

Exposure latitude is a measure of the margin for error available in this operation. It may be defined as the range of log E values through which the subject may be shifted while satisfactory reproduction is maintained (see Fig. 5.5). (Alternatively, latitude may be given in the form of an arithmetic ratio, in which case the range of log E values is the log latitude.) Thus if the subject luminance range exactly fills the useful exposure range, latitude is zero and the slightest exposure error will result in distortion of highlight or shadow tones, or in a negative whose quality is unacceptable because of excessive graininess. On the other hand, if the subject luminance range is narrow compared with the working range of the emulsion, latitude will be large and consequently exposure setting will be less critical.

Effects of Exposure Errors

Exposures lying outside the useful exposure range of the emulsion result in distorted densities in the negative which cannot be compensated for in printing. This is illustrated in Fig. 5.6, which shows the effects of exposure errors on the reproduction of a subject consisting of four tones, evenly spaced. In the case of *under-exposure,* the darker tones are so com-

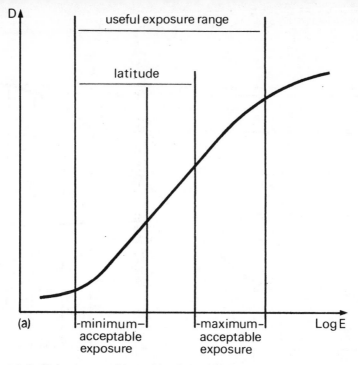

(a)

Fig. 5.5. *Latitude of an emulsion, with subject of (a) narrow and (b) wide luminance range*

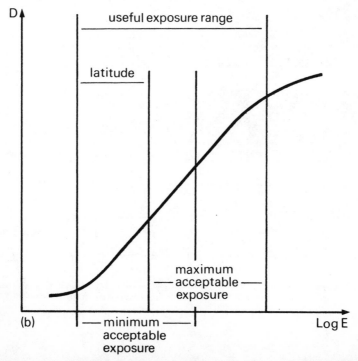

(b)

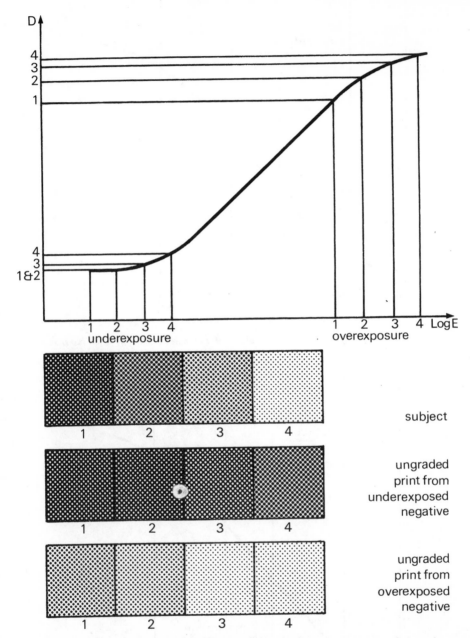

Fig. 5.6. Effects of exposure errors (for simplicity, the density of areas 3 and 4 in the print from the over-exposed negative has been taken to be identical)

pressed as to be indistinguishable in the negative, and it is obvious that no adjustment in printing will be able to restore the lost detail. In this particular case, exposures of both tones 1 and 2 have been less than the critical value of minimum useful exposure, with the result that not only are the subject areas indistinguishable from each other, but they also merge with the minimum density of the negative material itself, the fog level, and so do not constitute an image at all. *Over-exposure,* on the other hand, is the effect of placing the subject luminance range too far to the right, on the shoulder of the characteristic. In this case the highlight tones, 3 and 4, are recorded with such a minute difference in density that detail will inevitably be severely degraded, if not entirely lost, in the final print. Moreover, at this degree of exposure graininess will have reached a very high level, and detail will accordingly also be lost because of the low resolution of the image.

Printing Corrections

In motion picture photography it is important to maintain *lighting continuity,* i.e. key tones should be rendered by the same density in the positive image from shot to shot. This may be achieved by *grading,* which affects the overall density of the image as it is printed, and this is dealt with more fully in Chapter Seven. However it is important to realise at this stage that grading cannot restore photographic quality lost through initial under-exposure or over-exposure of the negative.

"Correct" Exposure of the Average Scene

Many experiments have been undertaken to discover what constitutes the "average" luminance range of a daylight subject. The significance of this is that it determines the calibration of light meters which indicate "correct" exposure settings from an integrated reading of the lighting conditions. In motion picture photography, the calculation of the average luminance range is complicated by the fact that we are dealing not with a single square or rectilinear composition but with a shot of indefinite length which by subject or camera movement may include areas of enormous contrast in luminance levels. Nevertheless conventional figures for the luminance range of an average sunlit scene have been arrived at, according to which the minimum luminance of the subject is, in the United Kingdom, 1.8 log E units, and in the United States 2.2 log E units less than the highlight maximum. These represent luminance ratios of 63:1 and 160:1 respectively. It is also possible to calculate the average luminance of the scene, which for the purpose of calibrated light meter readings corresponds with the luminance of a surface with average (18%) reflectance. Average luminance is fixed at 0.55 log E units less than the maximum.

Now within the useful exposure range of the emulsion, the optimum exposure of a subject is the minimum consistent with safety, since this yields the highest speed and the lowest graininess of which the emulsion is capable, given standard processing. With the above figures, we may thus illustrate the "correct" exposure for an average sunlit subject by reference to the speed point of the emulsion and incorporating 0.3 log E units as a safety factor (see Fig. 5.7). Typically, the exposure range of an average scene will fall partly on the upper portion of the toe and partly on the straight line of the characteristic.

For subjects whose ranges are longer or shorter than average, best results

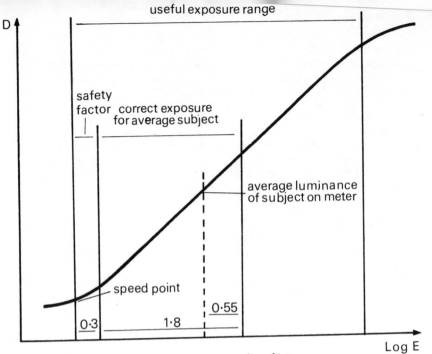

Fig. 5.7. "Correct" exposure of an average sunlit subject

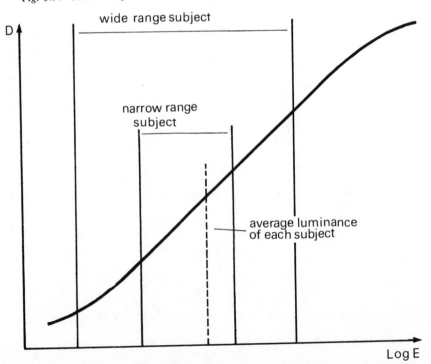

Fig. 5.8. "Correct" exposure of long-range and short-range subjects

are obtained by fixing the average luminance level at the same point as that of the average subject, and letting both the highlights and shadows be reproduced by densities differing proportionally from those of the average subject (see Fig. 5.8). This is the "key-tone pegging" method of exposure control, which ensures that flesh tones in particular are reproduced with consistency from shot to shot, a highly important consideration in motion picture photography.

In the case of an *excess luminance range,* subject range exceeds the useful exposure range of the emulsion even when flare is taken into account. This may occur, for example, in the case of strongly backlit scenes or when a single shot includes both interior and exterior luminance levels. Photographic distortion is then inevitable unless the luminance range can be reduced by means of fill light, etc.

The Effect of Development

The investigation of image formation and tone rendition has up to this point been carried out in terms of the type of emulsion used and the degree of exposure given, and standard processing has been assumed. It is next necessary to consider the effect of development.

If an emulsion is developed in a given solution at a fixed temperature for various lengths of time, a family of characteristic curves for the emulsion may be drawn (see Fig. 5.9). From these, various relationships concerning the effect of development on the characteristic of the film may be derived.

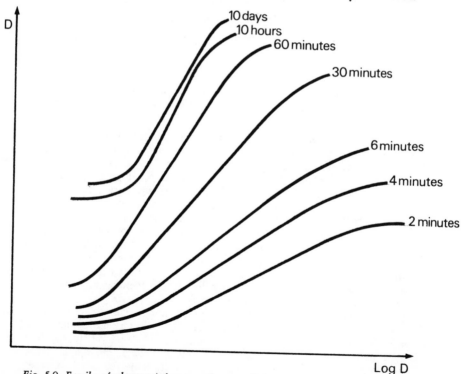

Fig. 5.9. Family of characteristic curves for a typical emulsion

Firstly, it may be seen that gamma rises steeply at first and then more slowly, reaching a maximum, after which it drops off. This accords with the effect of prolonging development time observed in Chapter Three and may be illustrated by a *gamma-time curve* (Fig. 5.10). Other properties of the

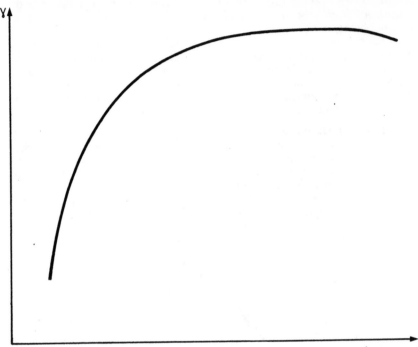

Fig. 5.10. Gamma-time curve

characteristic which vary with development time are emulsion speed and fog level. (Graininess is also affected, but since this is not indicated by characteristic curves discussion of this factor is deferred to Chapter Six.) Speed, like gamma, tends to increase with increased times of development, until after reaching a maximum it falls off. Fog level rises slowly until after a critical point it increases rapidly, making further development pointless.

The gamma-time, speed-time and fog-time curves for a hypothetical emulsion are combined in Fig. 5.11. It may be seen, for example, that a moderate gamma value is reached after a comparatively short time of development, and at this point speed is considerably below its maximum. If maximum speed were the preferred criterion, development time would need to be considerably extended, and the negative would then be very contrasty. Fog level, moreover, would then have risen appreciably.

In practice, as has been noted before, motion picture negatives are generally designed to be developed to a fixed gamma, 0.65. Thus if the gamma-time curve for a particular emulsion is drawn, the time of development required for a gamma of 0.65 may be read off directly. Moreover, the shape of the curve indicates how critically development time must be regulated in order

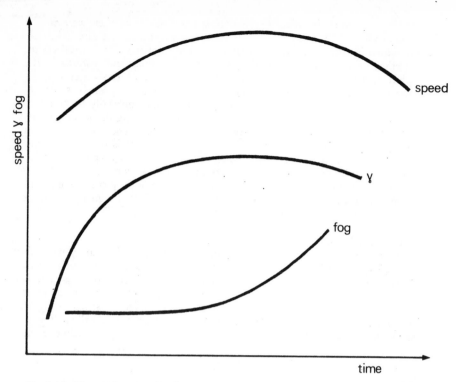

Fig. 5.11. Gamma-time, speed-time and fog-time curves of a typical emulsion

to achieve the desired gamma value: a steep curve indicates that the margin for error is very small. Gamma-temperature curves, with a similar profile, may also be constructed.

It is a usual procedure in still photography to vary development time (a) to compensate for exposure errors (b) to achieve desired high-contrast or low-contrast effects. Neither of these is generally practicable in motion picture work, where the laboratory practice of developing all negatives to a fixed gamma of 0.65 precludes the possibility of variations in development time (except in the case of "uprating," which is described below).

The basic reason for fixing the gamma value of negatives is that in motion picture work shots exposed and developed at widely differing times may be cut together into the final negative from which, usually by a duplicating process, release positives are to be printed. During printing, differences in contrastiness in the individual shots cannot be compensated for (unlike differences in density) since the positive strip must be developed throughout its length to a single gamma. For consistency in contrastiness in the final prints, therefore, each original negative shot must be developed to a fixed gamma.

The choice of a low value, 0.65, means that most film stocks have a comparatively wide useful exposure range and that mid-tones are well rendered in the negative. For the final print, the usual laboratory practice is aimed at creating a naturalistic effect by rendering tonal values as they were in the original subject. This requires an effective viewing gamma of approximately 1.0, which in turn necessitates, to allow for projector flare, screen reflections, the effect of viewing with a dark surround, etc., a final print gamma in the region of 1.3 to 1.6 (see Chapter Seven). A figure of this order may be achieved if negatives are printed on moderately contrasty positive stock.

It is evident, therefore, that exposure errors cannot normally be compensated for in development, though the possibility of grading the print permits a certain latitude which has been previously described. The other limitation imposed by the standard laboratory development practice is that special contrast effects desired for aesthetic reasons cannot generally be created by processing, although variable contrast release positive stocks are now being introduced (see Chapter Seven). Nevertheless, in motion picture work control of the contrast of the photographic image is best attained by careful regulation of subject illumination during shooting.

Uprating ("Pushing")

The procedure of *uprating* provides an exception to the laboratory methods described above, in that it does involve imparting a degree of development higher than that prescribed for the emulsion in question. The reason it is usually employed is, however, not to make up for random exposure errors or to achieve desired contrast effects but to increase the effective speed rating of the film stock. The results of overdevelopment (sometimes called "forced development" or "cooking") are shown in Fig. 5.12. The speed rating of the

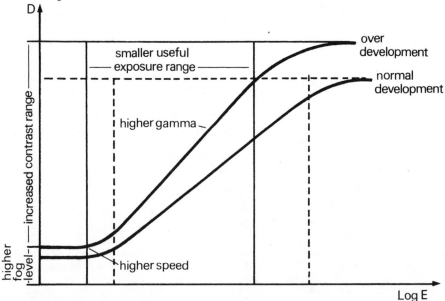

Fig. 5.12. Effects of overdevelopment

emulsion is increased, but at the expense of an increased fog level and a greater average grain size. Gamma is higher than normal, producing a more contrasty image associated with an increased contrast range and a smaller useful exposure range. Overdevelopment may be brought about by an increased time or temperature of development. Uprating or "pushing" a film stock consists of exposing the negative as if it had a higher speed rating and then subjecting it to overdevelopment by giving it the processing appropriate to a film with the higher rating. Thus, for example, a film with a daylight ASA speed of 400 could be rated at 800 ASA, its exposure halved with respect to normal levels, and its development intensified to the degree appropriate to an 800 ASA stock. Uprating is a useful method of obtaining passable photographic results in dim lighting conditions when faster stock is not available (and the subject luminance range is not wide). Because of its effect on contrast, fog level etc. in addition to speed, uprating is most successful when the complete sequence or film is shot in the same manner.

Underdevelopment produces results exactly opposite from those of "cooking." Since its beneficial effects—decreased fog level and graininess, for example—are more than counterbalanced by the loss of effective contrast and speed, it has little application in practical cinematography.

Tone Reproduction with Reversal Stocks

The exposure of reversal film is very much more critical than that of most negative stocks, and tone reproduction may easily be affected by small errors. This is because highlights in the subject should produce areas in the positive image which are just clear. Even slight over-exposure, which results in the bleaching away of too many grains, tends to produce washed-out highlights, while under-exposure causes the conversion of unaffected silver halides to a positive silver image, thus creating an unwanted density in the highlight area. To minimise the danger of too great a highlight density reversal emulsions are normally made very thin, which has the effect of increasing the potential contrast of the stock as well as reducing the useful exposure range.

Printing control by grading is possible when reversal originals are duplicated, but—for reasons discussed above—this by no means eliminates the necessity of very precise exposure estimation. The outstanding merit of reversal stocks is in minimising graininess, a subject which is treated in the next chapter.

Chapter VI
Grain Structure and Definition

A developed photographic image consists of microscopic grains of metallic silver dispersed in the gelatin binder of the emulsion. The grains are too small to be distinguished individually, since the largest are unlikely to be more than 3 to 5 micrometers—a micrometer or micron is a thousandth of a millimetre—in diameter. Varying densities in the image arise from the configuration of the exposed grains: they lie in differing degrees of concentration, at greater or lesser proximity to one another. This grouping occurs not only on a horizontal plane, but also vertically, throughout the thickness of the emulsion layer.

The important fact with which this chapter is concerned is that, even within an area of given (overall) density, the distribution of silver grains is *inhomogeneous*. This means that the grains are not evenly spaced in a geometrical arrangement, but instead located at random, with the result that there are minute irregularities in density over the given area. Scanning such an inhomogeneous field, the eye records the tiny density variations and the resulting signals to the brain give rise to a subjective impression of *graininess*.

The phenomenon of graininess is thus adequately explained by the random statistical distribution of grains in the emulsion layer, and the consequent non-uniformities within areas of given density. It is not necessary to postulate actual physical clumping, i.e. the formation of larger deposits of silver by the coalescence of individual grains, though in certain (unusual) circumstances this may in fact occur.

There is a rough correlation between the size of individual grains and the degree of magnification necessary before graininess becomes apparent. Normally a photographic image must be enlarged 50 diameters before separate grains can be distinguished, while a grainy pattern may emerge after magnifications of the order of 3 to 4 diameters. The effect of graininess in an image is to create a coarse appearance which destroys sharpness and clarity and hinders the rendering of fine detail. In motion pictures, the problem is somewhat alleviated by the fact that each frame has a distinct grain configuration and micro-irregularities in density thus tend to cancel themselves out over time. Nevertheless, the impression of "crawling" or "animated" grains which sometimes arises is highly unpleasant, and it is a major objective to reduce graininess to a minimum.

The Relationship between Graininess and Density

According to the statistical laws of random distribution, graininess in the sense of micro-irregularities in image density should slowly increase with increases in overall density, and this is in fact what happens. However the impression of graininess is also dependent upon image illumination: grain structure is more apparent to the observer in images or parts of an image which are brightly lit, i.e. areas of low density. These two factors might thus seem to cancel themselves out, but in the usual negative/positive process this is not so. Graininess is at a maximum in the heavily exposed portions of the negative, which are the areas of highest density. When the negative is printed, the grainy structure of these portions is transferred to the correspondingly lightly exposed areas of the positive image, which are the highlights of the picture. On projection, therefore, the actual graininess resulting from high densities in the negative is reinforced by better perception of graininess in the highlight areas. Consequently the effect of graininess is worst in large bright even-toned areas of the print, such as extensive sky regions. (Conversely, much night-for-night photography on fast, grainy stocks is acceptable because of the large shadow areas which predominate in the scene.) When reversal stock and processing are employed, however, the two factors do tend to cancel themselves out, with beneficial effect.

Factors Affecting Graininess

The major factors, apart from the density of the image, which affect the graininess of a print are as follows:

(a) *The sharpness of the camera image.* Since the part of the image which is sharply focussed in the camera renders detail well, graininess is less apparent in this area than in an out-of-focus portion.

(b) *The original emulsion grain-size distribution.* The most important factor in final print graininess is the average grain size of the original negative emulsion, which depends on the desired contrast and speed characteristics of the film (see Chapter Two).

(c) *The degree of exposure.* Since graininess increases with density, the degree of exposure greatly influences the grain structure of the image. Overexposure results in a rapid increase in graininess, and it is a general policy to make exposures as far towards the toe of the characteristic as possible.

(d) *The developing solution and the degree of development.* Generally, the more vigorous and lengthy the development, the larger the resulting average grain size.

(e) *The method of printing.* Graininess is substantially increased if specular, as opposed to diffuse light is used in printing (see Chapter Seven).

(f) *The grain-size distribution of the printing stock.* The graininess of the final print would of course be much increased if the positive stock employed had a grain-size distribution in any way approaching that of the original negative. For this reason all motion picture positive emulsions (and duplicating negatives) are extremely fine grained, and the influence of this factor is in practice almost negligible.

(g) *The viewing conditions.* Graininess is also dependent upon the degree of enlargement and the distance from which the print is viewed, grain structure being more apparent when the image is greatly enlarged and seen from a short distance. As mentioned above, the brightness of the image (in relation to ambient lighting) also affects the extent to which graininess is visible.

The Graininess of Reversal Stock

The factors listed above apply principally to prints produced by the negative/positive process. Special considerations arise in the case of reversal stock. When a reversal film is initially exposed, the grains affected are naturally the largest, since they are the most sensitive. During first development these grains are reduced to silver, and are then bleached away, leaving a potential positive image consisting of the smaller halide grains. Re-exposure and second development result in a silver image which is exceptionally fine grained by normal standards.

The Measurement of Graininess

Graininess was originally measured by a system of visual estimation, by means of which the photographic sample was given progressively higher degrees of magnification and numerical values were assigned according to the point at which graininess just became visible. This was a subjective method and required complicated control conditions with respect to illumination of the room in which viewing was made, etc. Moreover, it was difficult to plot graininess accurately against density because of the effect of image illumination on perception described above. The discovery that graininess was caused by micro-irregularities in image density led to the adoption of a new, objective method of measuring the manifestation of grain structure.

Granularity

Granularity is the term employed to designate inhomogeneity of the image as measured by an objective system, as distinct from subjectively-estimated graininess. Granularity is measured by taking a continuous series of micro-densitometer readings over a constant-density sample of the material to be tested. The readings are recorded in the form of a continuous line or *trace* (see Fig. 6.1), and if the readings were constant—if, that is, the photo-

Fig. 6.1. Microdensitometer trace

graphic image was uniform throughout—the trace would consist of a straight horizontal line. Irregularities in the microdensitometer trace represent deviations from the density norm, and statistical analysis enables a measurement of granularity to be derived from the standard deviation. A factor which must be taken into account in this calculation is the aperture of the microdensitometer, since the wider the beam of light, the greater the tendency to even out departures from the mean density. In practice a scanning spot whose diameter is 10 to 20 times that of the average grain size is found to be most satisfactory, while the influence of aperture size on the results is cancelled out by multiplying the deviation figure by the square root of the area of the scanning spot. The constant figure thus obtained is referred to as the "root-mean-square" or "RMS" granularity. It may be combined with others derived from the same material at different densities, producing a graph as in Fig. 6.2. The microdensitometer technique permits precise measurement and is a crucial tool in the study of image grain structure.

Resolving Power

The ability of an emulsion to render fine detail well is termed its *resolving power*. The chief factors influencing resolving power include:

(a) *The contrast ratio of the subject.* Best performance of an emulsion in terms of resolving power is obtained from a subject having a high contrast ratio within the area in which fine detail is to be distinguished.

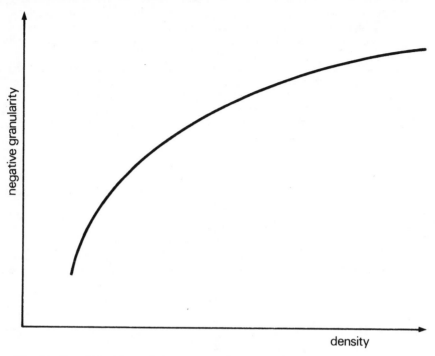

Fig. 6.2. Granularity of a typical negative stock

(b) *The resolving power of the lens.* Poor resolution encountered in photographic work often results from limitations in the resolving power of the lens rather than the emulsion. For test purposes, the performance of the lens should be at least 3 times that of the film.

(c) *The wavelength of the exposing light.* Resolving power tends to increase as the wavelength of the emulsion decreases, i.e. as the colour of the subject or the light source varies from the red to the blue end of the spectrum.

(d) *The degree of exposure.* Resolving power rises steadily to a maximum as exposure increases, and then just as steadily falls off. Under-exposure and over-exposure thus tend to produce very poor resolution.

(e) *The graininess of the emulsion.* This is the most significant factor in resolving power, and in general a fine-grain emulsion automatically has a high resolving power. There are, however, exceptions to this rule, and there are development techniques which will favour either the formation of a fine-grain image or resolving power, but not both.

(f) *The thickness of the emulsion layer.* Resolving power is diminished as a result of the scattering of light by the grains in the emulsion, causing irradiation. The thicker the emulsion coating, the worse this effect becomes.

(g) *The type of developer.* Usually fine-grain developing solutions favour the formation of an image with high resolving power, but this is not necessarily so in all cases. The alkali employed in the developing solution may have a significant effect. With a typical borax developer, for example, resolving power reaches a maximum only after several minutes of development, when gamma has attained a comparatively high value; while with the use of a developer of a different constitution resolving power may be at its maximum as development commences and fall steadily as it is prolonged.

(h) *Gamma and time of development.* While a contrasty image, considered in itself, has a high potential resolving power, the effect of extending development time and thus attaining a higher gamma is counteracted by the concomitant increase in graininess. Thus, depending on the type of developer (see above), resolving power generally reaches a maximum soon after development has commenced and then falls off at a slower or faster rate.

The Measurement of Resolving Power

Measuring resolving power is a simple procedure: some writers have suggested it is deceptively simple. The technique used is to photograph at a high degree of reduction a test chart consisting of a pattern of sets of parallel dark lines on a light background or vice versa, the space between the lines being equal in width to the lines themselves, and the size of the sets steadily diminishing (see Fig. 6.3). The negative derived after standard processing is examined under a microscope, and it is possible to determine with a fair degree of accuracy the point at which lines cannot be distinguished from one

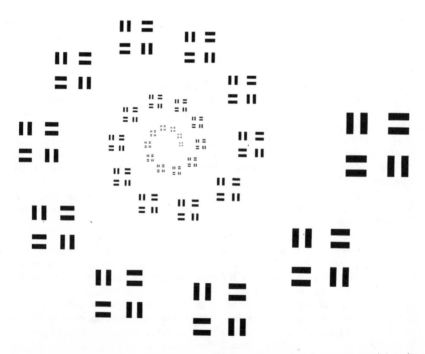

Courtesy Research Laboratories, Kodak Ltd.

Fig. 6.3. Typical resolving power test chart (contrast 1000:1)

another, i.e. are not resolved. The results may be expressed in terms of the number of lines per millimetre which the emulsion is capable of resolving. The resolving power of various emulsions (for a high contrast test chart) lie approximately in the following ranges:

Motion picture negative (fast) .... 40– 60 lines/mm
Motion picture negative (medium speed) ...... 70–100 lines/mm
Motion picture positive .... 120–200 lines/mm

It is important to recognise that comparable tests must be made at the same exposure.

The relationship between resolving power and relative exposure for test objects with different contrast ratios may be shown in a graph such as Fig. 6.4, and the effect of development time on resolving power, compared with gamma, for a highspeed emulsion in a borax developer by a diagram such as Fig. 6.5.

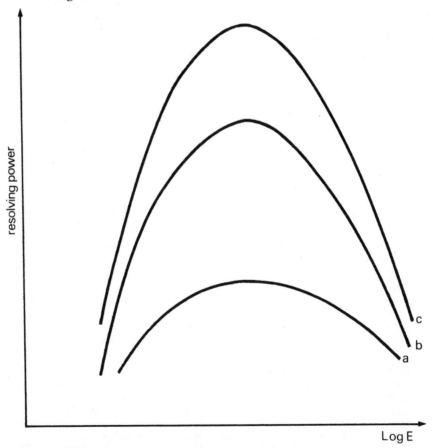

Fig. 6.4. Relationship between resolving power (lines/mm) and relative log exposure using test objects having a contrast ratio of (a) 2:1 (b) 8:1 (c) 1000:1, for a typical emulsion

79

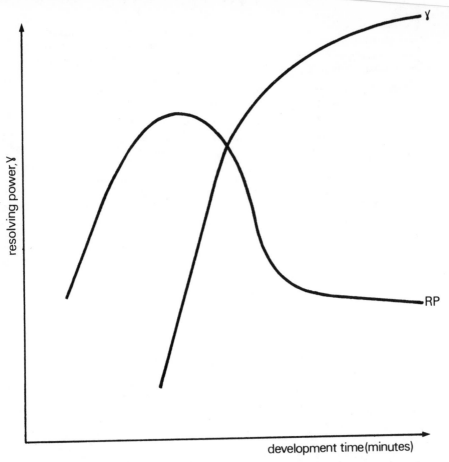

Fig. 6.5. Effect of development time on resolving power as compared with gamma, for a high speed emulsion in a borax developer

The Limitations of the Resolving Power Criterion

The resolving power of an emulsion is an important consideration in astronomical photography, spectrography, etc. But as a criterion for determining the sharpness of the image which an emulsion is capable of producing in normal pictorial motion picture photography, resolving power has been subjected to considerable criticism. This is because it is based on a threshold measurement, and the detail which is involved at this point even with coarse-grained emulsions is considerably smaller than that which can be distinguished by the naked eye. There is no direct correlation between resolving power and the clarity of a photographic image as it appears to the ordinary observer. Moreover, resolving power tests are usually carried out on high contrast charts, but when the resolution of detail is crucial the subject is often of low contrast. For the purposes of *photographic definition,* or the sharpness with which details are reproduced in normal viewing conditions, a more important criterion is found to be *acutance.*

Acutance

A term which was previously introduced in the discussion of development techniques, *acutance*—the objective equivalent of "sharpness"—is defined as the steepness of the density gradient at an abrupt boundary between lightly-exposed and heavily-exposed areas in the negative. This may be illustrated by a consideration of the exposure of a film which is partially shielded by a knife-edge (see Fig. 6.6). The ideal film would reproduce the boundary by a vertical increase in density, but in fact the response of any practical film is graduated (see Fig. 6.7).

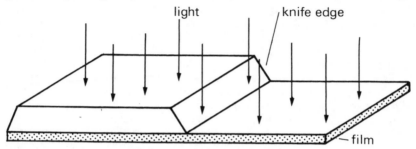

Fig. 6.6. Exposure of film partially shielded by a knife-edge

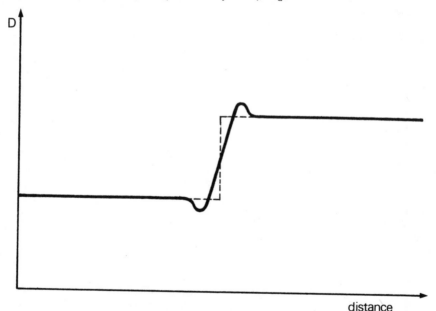

Fig. 6.7. Response of an ideal film (dotted line) and practical film (solid line) to exposure at a knife-edge boundary

The practical density contour demonstrates the effect of irradiation, which was briefly discussed in Chapter Two. Irradiation occurs as a result of *turbidity,* or the property of the emulsion by which light is diffused into regions which have received no direct exposure, and hence causes the reduction of silver halide grains beyond the image area. *Optical turbidity* refers to the sideways reflection, refraction, diffraction etc. of the light striking the emulsion, and depends on the wavelength of the light, the degree of exposure, the thickness and grain-size distribution of the emulsion layer, the halide to gelatin ratio, and related factors, most of which have already been discussed as affecting the film's resolving power. *Photographic turbidity* describes the manner in which light intensities are converted into densities in the silver image, and depends on the shape of the emulsion characteristic and in particular the gamma to which the film is developed: a contrasty film produces steeper density contours and hence sharper images.

Acutance and resolving power tend, to a certain extent, to go together, since they are both favoured by fine-grained emulsions and factors which restrict irradiation. But beyond the point at which detail ceases to be discernible by the naked eye, techniques which increase resolving power may militate against acutance, since they facilitate the rendering of excessive detail which for maximum image sharpness is best eliminated in favour of sharper differentiation between larger and more important image areas. Acutance may also be increased by edge or adjacency effects, described in Chapter Three, which actually intensify significant dividing lines in the image. In practical motion picture photography, a film which has been developed to give maximum acutance is found to provide better definition than one processed for maximum resolving power.

The Measurement of Acutance

Acutance is measured by recording increments in density over the boundary region by means of a microdensitometer trace. Plotted on a graph against distance, the trace resembles the solid-line contour in Fig. 6.7. However to

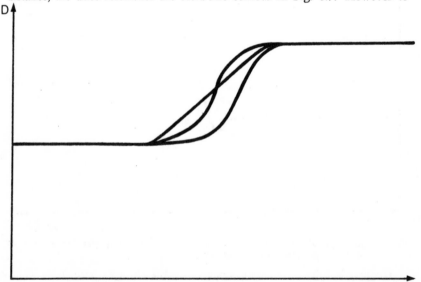

Fig. 6.8. Reproduction of a knife-edge by three different emulsions (disregarding edge effects)

attain a numerical value for acutance it is not sufficient merely to calculate the gradient or average gradient of the boundary contour, for three different emulsions (for example) may reproduce a knife-edge with the same initial and final densities, over the same distance and with the same average gradient, but nevertheless produce very different impressions of sharpness (see Fig. 6.8). A mathematical technique has therefore been devised which requires the derivation, from a large number of point or sectional gradient measurements, of a figure denoting the "mean value of the gradient squared." This is then divided by the "density scale" which is the difference between two densities at a certain gradient value. The method enables very accurate calculations of acutance to be made, which accord in all but exceptional cases with the subjective impression of image sharpness formed by an observer.

Modulation Transfer

The drawbacks of using resolving power as the criterion for image sharpness have already been discussed. Even when a measure of a film's ability to render ultra-fine detail is required, resolving power may be misleading. *Modulation transfer* or *sine wave response* is a technique now widely employed in calculating the resolution which a lens, film or lens-film combination is capable of achieving.

The *modulation transfer function* (MTF) of a film is arrived at by photographing a test object with a sinusoidal pattern, like that for example illustrated in Fig. 6.9. If the density of the developed image of each section of

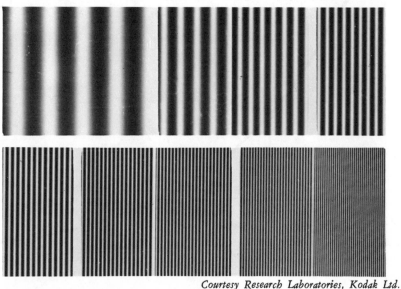

Courtesy Research Laboratories, Kodak Ltd.

Fig. 6.9. Portion of an MTF Sine-Wave Test Object

the test object is then plotted against distance, the curve indicating the response of the emulsion will appear as in Fig. 6.10. Now the vertical amplitude, or (doubled) the density range of this response curve depends on

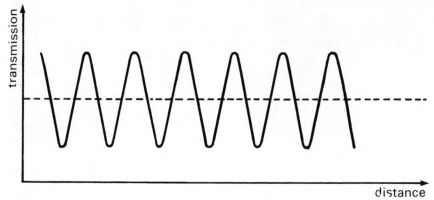

Fig. 6.10. *Variation of transmission with distance along photographic image of MTF test object at a given frequency*

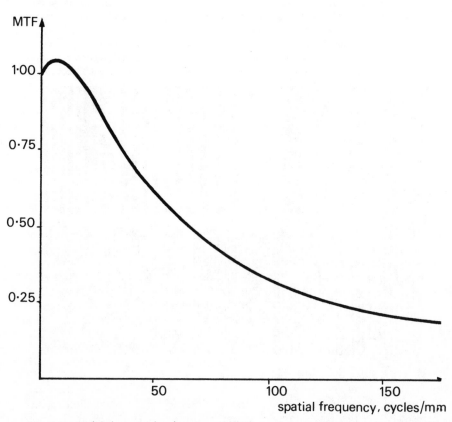

Fig. 6.11. *Modulation transfer function (MTF) or sine-wave response of a typical emulsion*

the spatial frequency of the test pattern. If the light and dark areas of the test object are sufficiently spread out, the contrast will be accurately recorded on the film in accordance with its D log E characteristic and modulation transfer is said to be 100%. (If edge effects operate, the figure may in fact exceed 100%.) However as the spatial frequency of the test object increases, and the pattern is condensed, the emulsion has an increasing tendency to average out light and dark areas and the full contrast range of the original is not reproduced. The modulation transfer function is defined as the ratio Mi/Mo, where Mi is the modulation of the developed image, and Mo the modulation of the test object measured at the film (since the lens employed also affects the performance of the photographic system).

If the MTF is calculated for a number of different spatial frequencies of the test object, a curve such as that in Fig. 6.11 may be derived. The function is a very sensitive indicator of edge effects, which may cause values in excess of 1.0 to be recorded at low spatial frequencies. It is also easy to gauge the resolution which may be expected at any given degree of detail. Moreover, since modulation transfer curves can be easily combined, it is possible to predict with accuracy the effect of changing a component—a film stock or printer, for example—in a system such as that used in duplicating and printing motion picture film.

Chapter VII
Printing

Printing is the method by which photographic images are reproduced. For motion picture purposes, the material on to which printing is carried out is film stock on (normally) triacetate base similar to that of the original negative or positive master, having, however, rather different emulsion characteristics. The operation is performed on a printing machine or *printer* which shines light through the original, exposing the copy film in the appropriate areas. The intensity of light transmitted by the original is naturally dependent upon the density of the image, being high where density is low and vice versa, and this accounts for the reversed tonalities in film printed by the monochrome negative/positive process. Reversal originals may be printed either on to negative or on to reversal printing stock. The exposed emulsion is then developed and fixed as usual.

In motion picture work printing procedure is normally as follows. The original camera negatives of the day's shooting are developed and from them *rush prints* ("rushes" or "dailies") are taken. These are edited as the *work print* or *cutting copy*, which eventually forms the pattern for cutting the original negative. The edited negative is then used for the production of *release* or *projection* prints, either directly or via an intermediate process, which normally involves the printing of a *fine-grain master positive* and one or more *duplicating* or *dupe negatives*. In a recently developed printing procedure for colour, the two duplicating stages are telescoped into one by means of a *colour reversal intermediate* stock. When sound and picture are combined in synchronisation on the same piece of film, the process is sometimes referred to as *married printing* and the resultant copy as a *married print*.

Even when only a few release prints are required, a dupe negative is often made as an insurance measure and to avoid the danger of damage to the original. A *duplicate cutting copy* or "slash print" may be made from the rushes (via an intermediate negative) at a relatively advanced stage of editing for purposes such as exhibition to producers or sponsors. The term *answer print* (or *trial composite*) generally refers to a print struck from the edited original and submitted to the producers for their acceptance. Once a satisfactory answer print has been made, it is the task of the laboratory to duplicate it as closely as possible in density, contrast, colour balance and other characteristics in all subsequent release prints.

Types of Printer

The quality of the final image may be affected by the type of machine used in making the print. The two basic methods in the motion picture industry are *contact printing*, in which the negative and positive films are placed in contact with each other, and *optical printing*, whereby the image is transferred by means of a lens system.

Contact printing is the simpler and cheaper technique and is less affected by dirt, dust and scratches on the master. There is a danger, however, of interference patterns ("Newton's rings") being produced if the two film surfaces are in uneven contact and thus not mutually parallel. Optical printing

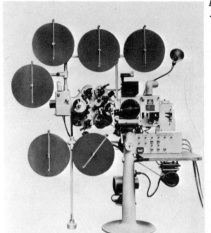

Fig. 7.1. SOS/Takita Model CP-2100 continuous-contact printer

Courtesy SOS Photo-Cine-Optics Inc.

Fig. 7.2. Sound and picture heads of the Bell & Howell Model C continuous-contact printer

Courtesy
Filmatic
Laboratories

Fig. 7.4. *SOS/Takita Model OP-5100 optical reduction and step-contact printer*

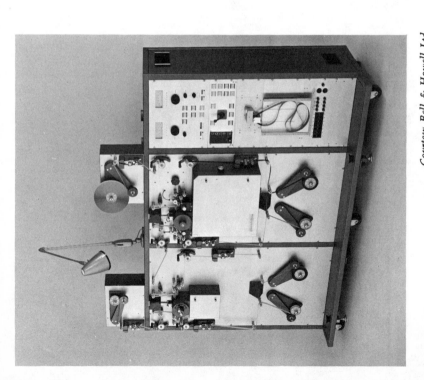

Fig. 7.3. *Bell & Howell panel printer. This advanced machine is of the continuous-contact type and prints film at the rate of 240 ft. per minute.*

is necessary when there is to be any change in the shape or size of the resultant frame, e.g. in *reduction printing* from 35mm to 16mm or in "blowing up" a 35mm original to 70mm; when anamorphic squeezing or unsqueezing in printing is required; when there is to be a modification in frame sequence, e.g. freeze frames and "stretch" printing; and for other effects such as optical zooms and travelling mattes (see below).

Contact printers may be of the *continuous* (rotary) or *intermittent* (step) type. In the case of the continuous-contact printer, there is danger of slippage, with consequent loss in image clarity and resoluton. Slippage is aggravated by film shrinkage, since the master film is already processed—which tends to shorten the film slightly— and the copy film unprocessed. In an attempt to minimise this problem, the printer gate is curved with the unprocessed film running on the outside. Intermittent-contact printers avert the danger of slippage by advancing the films frame by frame as in a camera. They are slower and in general more accurate than the continuous type, and are invariably used when a high degree of image resolution is essential.

Optical printers are almost universally of the intermittent type, except for the purpose of printing optical sound tracks. In this last case continuous machines are necessary, a frame-by-frame mechanism being obviously unsuitable. Problems of shrinkage are again encountered and are manifested in a small degree of wow and flutter.

A major factor influencing the quality of the printed image is the degree to which illumination of the films at the printer gate is specular or diffuse. It is a situation in which a compromise is necessary. A highly specular printer light produces an image which is very sharp, but also very grainy. This is because light from a highly directional source is scattered very little by the emulsion grains and thus micro-irregularities in image density are maximised. Diffuse illumination, on the other hand, by evening out the exposure given to the grains in the printing emulsion, results in a less grainy as well as softer image.

In optical printers the problem of striking a compromise is particularly acute. It is difficult to incorporate lamps of sufficient intensity, and diffusion may result in the loss of anything from 50% to 90% of light from the original source. Very specular light in an optical printer, however, causes every mark, scratch or speck on the negative or lens elements to be reproduced on the print film. Moreover, a very highly specular source can produce unpleasant edge effects such as, in colour, yellow lines around the blacks. One method of effecting a compromise sometimes practised is to use specular light when printing on to negative stock, to obtain the sharpest possible results, and diffuse light for making positives suitable for projection.

The effect of scratches on the film from which printing is being done may be minimised by the use of a *liquid gate* (see Fig. 7.5). If no preventative measures are taken, light from the printer striking a scratch in the base of the film is refracted, with the result that areas in the print are correspondingly under- and over-exposed. If, however, the film is surrounded by a transparent liquid whose refractive index is similar to that of the acetate base or gelatin (in practice a compromise figure is often chosen) light striking the film surface will not be refracted no matter what the angle of incidence. The liquid chosen must not, of course, contain water, or it will be absorbed by the gelatin of the emulsion.

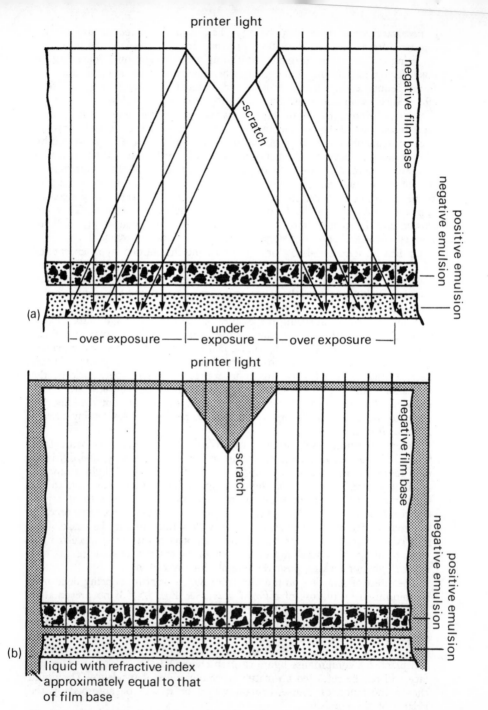

Fig. 7.5. *Effect of scratches in the negative film base (a) in a standard printer (b) in a liquid gate printer*

Characteristics of Printing Stock

The characteristics of the three main types of black-and-white film stock employed in printing processes—fine-grain duplicating positive, dupe negative and release positive—are outlined below.

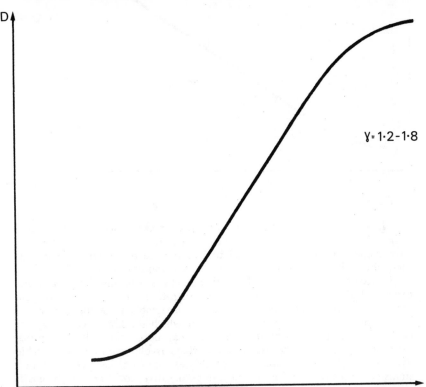

Fig. 7.6. Characteristic of a fine-grain positive duplicating stock

(a) *Fine-grain positive.* For producing master copies from the original negative, fine-grain positive stocks (Fig. 7.6), in common with other duplicating materials, are very slow with a high potential definition. They are moderately contrasty, having a recommended gamma of from 1.2 to 1.8. Fine-grain positive films are not normally colour-sensitised, and thus may be dyed yellow to absorb a certain percentage of the blue exposing light and thereby help prevent loss of detail by irradiation. For special purposes, such as printing a black-and-white master positive from an original colour negative, they may be panchromatic.

(b) *Duplicating ("dupe") negative.* Dupe negative stocks (Fig. 7.7) are used in the intermediate printing stage between fine-grain master positives and the final release prints. They are very slow, fine grained, and generally panchromatic (though blue-sensitive only stocks are available) and are designed to be developed to the same gamma as the original negative, i.e. generally 0.65.

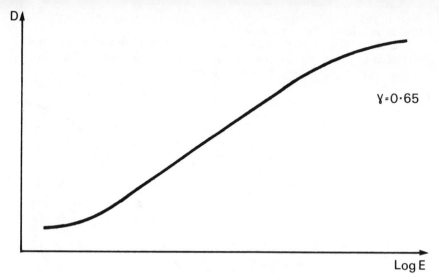

$\gamma = 0.65$

Fig. 7.7. *Characteristic of a dupe negative stock*

(c) *Release positive.* Like other printing stocks, release positive films (Fig. 7.8) are slow and fine grained. They are very contrasty, having a recommended gamma of about 2.2 to 2.6, and are not usually colour-sensitised, although panchromatic stocks are now beginning to be introduced.

The recommended gamma of printing stocks is determined by the overall gamma of the system (see below). In order to minimise graininess, print films are invariably slow in speed: this is acceptable since the intensity of illumination in the printer and the rate at which the films pass the printer gate are under full control and exposure may be considerably higher than for camera negatives. The use of stock which is blue-sensitive only enables red safelights to be employed, though this may restrict the speed of certain emulsions excessively and hence most dupe negative stocks are panchromatic.

Grading

All printers have some means of controlling the exposure which is given to the print film. Some types of high speed printers designed specifically for dupe negatives are adjustable only at the beginning of a print run, but most printers incorporate a mechanism to vary exposure as frequently as desired while the machine is operating, and thus individual shots may be *graded* or *timed,* i.e. given the degree of exposure necessary to maintain lighting continuity throughout the film. The time of exposure may be modulated in continuous printers by altering the width of the slit aperture, while intermittent printers may incorporate a variable shutter. Alternatively, the intensity of the light source may be adjusted by means of an iris diaphragm in the path of the beam or, for black-and-white prints only, a rheostat in the lamp circuit.

Grading affects the overall density of the image, or more precisely the series of adjacent frame images which constitute the shot. (Attempts are sometimes made to vary exposure within a single shot, but this is a rare and difficult procedure: normally grading is done on a shot-by-shot basis.) It might be thought that a photo-electric device measuring light transmission

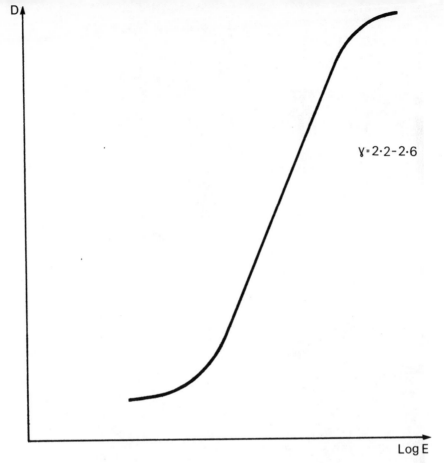

$\gamma = 2\cdot2 - 2\cdot6$

Fig. 7.8. Characteristic of a release positive stock

could be invented to regulate automatically the exposure given and bring each shot to an average level. In fact this is not so, since lighting continuity depends not on the average illumination of the scene but the lighting of a key area within it. The choice of what constitutes this key area is a subjective decision which no machine is capable of taking. Moreover, the key area, the illumination of which determines the exposure setting for the complete shot, may in fact occupy only a small fraction of the image area. A leading player, for example, might be seen initially in long shot, as only one object among many, and in the next shot in close-up, dominating the image. Lighting continuity might well require the illumination of his face to be constant from the first shot to the second, but an automatic instrument would be incapable of the requisite discrimination between picture areas. In addition, a photo-electric cell system could make allowances for the lighting styles of individual cameramen only in the crudest manner. Grading is thus a subjective process, and the quality of results depends upon the skill, experience and judgement of the *grader* or *timer*.

Courtesy Filmatic Laboratories

Fig. 7.9. Tape punch and verifier for coding light changes on the Bell & Howell Model C printer

Courtesy Rank Organisation

Fig. 7.10. The pre-punched control tape is read by the printer

The stage at which a graded print is first produced depends upon the number of copies of the original being printed. If a few release prints are being taken from the original negative, each of these must be given the necessary light changes during printing. If there is to be only a single dupe negative, this normally becomes the first graded print, but in the case of more than one dupe negative grading corrections may be incorporated in the master positive, in which event all subsequent prints whether negative or positive will be automatically correct without the need for further exposure adjustments.

A *printer light setting control* on the printer allows exposure to be varied along a graduated scale with a fixed number of steps, each of which changes the log exposure by a given amount. Printer light settings are relative and consistent only within a given laboratory. The grader judges the exposure to be given each shot after viewing the film and occasionally has the aid of "Cinex strips." These are test strips of a number of adjacent frames from a given shot subjected, on a device known as a *motion picture timer,* to exposures equivalent to printer light settings. They are placed after development against a lighted panel on which each shot of the sequence and average scenes from the film may be compared; there is a danger, however, that the exposures given to the Cinex strips will not correspond with absolute accuracy to the characteristics of the particular printer to be used. Cinex strips are generally not employed in 16mm work.

On major productions, a *grading conference* will be held at which the grader confers with personnel such as the producer, director, editor and cameraman as to the overall lighting continuity required. Decisions on smaller productions will frequently be left entirely to the grader. The grader draws up a programme for the printer which may be altered after the first run if necessary, or maintained intact for the production of further identical prints.

Exposure Errors

As was pointed out in Chapter Five, grading cannot compensate for exposure errors which place the subject outside the useful exposure range of the emulsion. Fig. 7.11 illustrates the way in which grading to an average density would affect the prints from the badly-exposed subject indicated without correction in Fig. 5.6 (p. 66). While the predominant heavy and light densities of the under-exposed and over-exposed prints respectively may both be adjusted to an average grey, tone separation remains very poor and neither the highlights nor the shadow areas of the original subject are reproduced with any degree of fidelity.

Optical Effects ("Opticals")

Optical printers consist of two basic components, a "projector" which transports the film to be copied through the *printer head,* where it is illuminated from the rear by a powerful lamp, and a "camera" with a lens system which focusses the master film image and photographs it frame by frame on to a copy film stock. The master and copy films are normally a fine-grain positive and dupe negative respectively, and are so referred to in this section. Because the two films are transported independently of each other, frame synchronisation being achieved by an interlock system which does not impede the printer's flexibility, an extremely wide variety of special

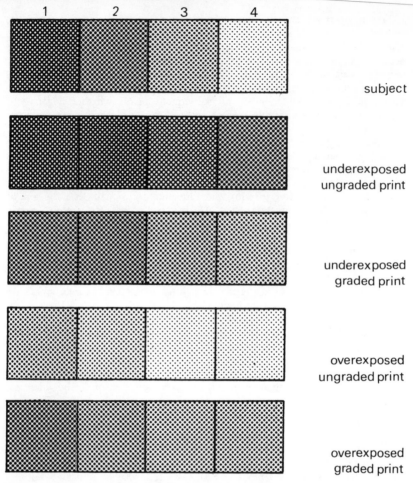

Fig. 7.11. *Effects of grading badly-exposed prints*

effects is possible. These effects are achieved by means of the following basic techniques, alone or in combination:

(a) *Printer light modification.* As in other types of printer, the intensity of the light source may be made to vary, usually by the use of a shutter. By gradually increasing or decreasing the light, *fade-ins* and *fade-outs* of virtually any length may be produced.

(b) *Multiple runs.* After the duplicating film has been exposed once, it may be re-wound and re-exposed to a different length of master positive. Assuming appropriate exposure calculations are made, this process may be repeated an indefinite number of times, resulting in *superimpositions*. A superimposed fade-out and fade-in is termed a *dissolve. Travelling mattes* are systems by which composite pictures are obtained by combining film of the main subject with live action or painted, modelled, etc. backgrounds shot at a different time. The usual method by which the components of a travelling matte shot

Courtesy Rank Organisation

Fig. 7.12. Optical printers at Denham Laboratories. Uses include reduction printing and anamorphic conversions.

are synthesised, in professional motion picture work, is by a multiple run in the optical printer.

(c) *Modification of the relative film speeds.* The films in the projector and camera may be made to move at virtually any speed in relation to each other; to stop and start, skipping or repeating according to a programmed frame sequence; to move in opposite directions. The effects possible by this means include *freeze frames,* when a single frame is duplicated a number of times by holding it stationary in the printer head; *fast motion,* when frames in the fine-grain are omitted at predetermined intervals; and a type of *slow motion,* when frames in the master are repeated according to a formula. This variety of slow motion effect differs from that achieved when, in original shooting of a moving subject, film is run through the camera at a faster speed than normal and each frame, being taken at a very short interval following the previous one, is distinct. The optical printer method tends to produce jerkiness in action, and is inferior for most purposes.

By gradually increasing or decreasing the number and frequency of frames which are repeated or skipped, *acceleration* and *deceleration* of action may be brought about. *Pixillation,* or the apparent jerky animation of persons or objects, is made possible by a combination of skip-frame and multiple-frame printing. A specialised application of the technique is *stretch printing,* or adapting silent films shot at 16 frames per second (f.p.s.) for sound projection at 24 f.p.s. The usual method is to repeat every second frame in the

97

master, so that the sequence becomes 1,2,2,3,4,4,5,6,6, etc. Finally, by running the film in the camera in the opposite direction from that in the projector, *reverse action* is attainable.

(d) *Modification of the distance between, and alignment of the projector, lens and camera.* In a typical optical printer, the camera and the lens, with an extension bellows and tube, may be moved toward or away from the projector head and each other by being mounted in a geared bed. In some printers, the camera or projector may also be moved laterally and vertically and tilted through several degrees around its optical axis. The basic effects made possible by these movements are changes in image size and position on the dupe negative frame. Thus *magnification* of a particular portion of the original is possible, a gradual enlargement being termed an *optical zoom.* *Reduction* is equally feasible, and when combined with multiple runs and appropriate modifications in positioning on the copy frames, *multiple image* effects may be achieved. Artificial *addition of motion*—to simulate for example the rocking of a boat—is possible, as also are certain *salvaging* operations involving the removal of unwanted camera shake, etc. In combination with a double run, again, these movements of the printer components relative to each other may be used to create a *push-off,* in which one shot appears to take over from another by forcing it off the screen vertically, horizontally or diagonally. Alteration of the lens position may be used to create any *out-of-focus* effect desired, often in connection with dissolves.

(e) *Interposing of special lenses and filters, spin attachments and wipe attachments.* The variety of effects which may be achieved by distorting or masking the transmitted image is very wide indeed. A standard procedure is carrying out the *anamorphic conversions*—squeezing or unsqueezing in the correct ratio—required by the various wide screen systems. These are done by inserting the requisite anamorphic lens in the light path. Lenses of similar design may occasionally be used for special distortion effects, *elongation* or *shrinking* of the image, etc. *Kaleidoscopic* effects, appearing as shattered and multiplied images, are also possible with the appropriate lens. *Ripple* and *diffusion* are attained by inserting special filters. Images of a different quality result from the use of a transparent *texture screen.*

An optical spin attachment mounted between the projector and the camera enables *rotary movements* and *spiral effects* (including *spin-ins* and *spin-outs*) to be achieved, and combined with a multiple run makes possible vertical or horizontal *flip-overs* as transitional devices. A mechanical spin attachment mounted in the printer head in place of the intermittent advance mechanism may alternatively be used for some of these effects, though continuing motion within the frame is then no longer possible.

Another feature of the optical printer is the wipe attachment. This consists of a mounting for a blade or combination of blades which may be mechanically or automatically adjusted to obscure a growing or diminishing area of the image in a series of repeatable frame-by-frame steps. With a double run and precise calibration of the blade movements, the device may be used to produce the familiar *wipe* from one scene to another. (This differs from the push-off in that the images themselves do not move across the screen.) Laboratories can normally offer a variety of different wipe designs from their catalogue. The wipe edge can be made harder or softer by altering the distance of the blade from the lens. The wipe device, fitted with fixed or moving mattes and counter-mattes, may also be used to produce various *split screen* effects. Like travelling mattes, and unlike multiple image effects, these are generally designed to obscure the manipulation which is involved. Some of the possibilities include the playing of dual roles by a single actor, the removal of unwanted moving objects or people from a shot, the juxtaposition of actors and dangerous animals, and the bringing of human beings closer to explosions, burning buildings etc.

(f) *Replacement of whole or part of the projector and/or camera. Reduction printing* and *blowing up* from one gauge to another are made possible by making the appropriate change in the equipment used. In some cases it is not necessary to remove and replace the complete projector or camera, but only certain parts of the transport mechanism.

A and B Roll Printing

A method of printing in two runs from a negative or reversal original edited into two separate rolls is in widespread use in 16mm work and is beginning to be used in 35mm. The technique is to alternate shots from one roll to the other in checkerboard fashion, gaps being filled with black leader. Occasionally three or more rolls might be necessary for certain effects, such as superimposition over a dissolve in title sequences. The A and B roll printing method has the following advantages:

(a) Prints containing fades, dissolves and superimpositions may be produced directly from the original, thus avoiding the loss of quality in duplication which is particularly noticeable in 16mm.

(b) Splice marks which may otherwise become visible in 16mm printing are eliminated.

(c) Costs are cut on small numbers of prints.

The disadvantages are basically:

(a) Only standard length fades and dissolves are possible. Laboratories can usually offer effects of 16, 24, 32, 48, 64 or 96 frames in length.

(b) Extra work and expense is involved in negative cutting and printing.

(c) For a large number of prints the A and B roll method is less economical than obtaining optical effects by duplication in the usual way.

(d) Only black titles may be superimposed when working with negative, and white titles with reversal original.

Vesicular Printing Stock and Processing

When a conventional black-and-white film is projected, images are formed on the screen because part of the projection light is *absorbed* by grains of metallic silver. Recent research has led to the development of a revolutionary printing stock in the emulsion of which silver grains are supplanted by tiny cavities or "vesicles" which form an image by *scattering* light (see Fig. 7.13).

The basis of the Kalvar process (developed by Metro/Kalvar Inc.) is an emulsion consisting of thermoplastic resin within which molecules of a compound sensitive to ultra-violet light are uniformly dispersed. Upon exposure to a source such as a mercury-vapour lamp, the photo-sensitive molecules decompose to form bubbles of nitrogen and other volatile products which constitute the "latent image." The film is then "developed" by subjecting it to a heat treatment. This causes the gaseous decomposition products to expand and the crystallites to soften, with the result that vesicles ranging from 0.5 to 2

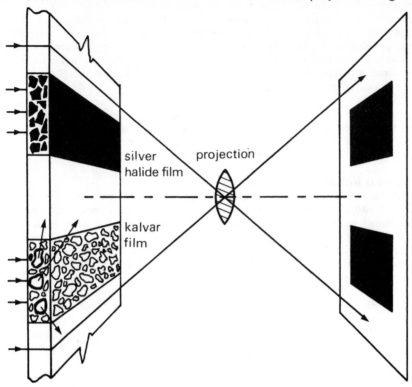

section of emulsion viewed projected images

silver halide film

projection

kalvar film

Courtesy Metro/Kalvar Inc.

Fig. 7.13. Reproduction of an image by conventional and vesicular methods

micrometers in diameter are formed in the thermoplastic emulsion layer. "Fixing" is then carried out by uniformly exposing the emulsion to ultra-violet light, which neutralises the remaining photo-sensitive molecules.

The vesicles thus constitute a positive image in a similar manner to the grains of metallic silver suspended in gelatin of the traditional emulsion. The important distinction is that they scatter light incident upon them at a sharp angle, ensuring that it does not strike the screen. Scattering occurs because the refractive index of the vesicles differs from that of the surrounding medium.

Vesicular emulsions are not suitable for original camera negative stocks, firstly because they are comparatively slow and secondly because they are sensitive only to ultra-violet light. (The range in fact extends from approximately 350nm–430nm, or into the deep blue-violet region, but the emulsions are not sensitive to normal levels of visible light for comparatively short periods.) But for black-and-white printing, the new emulsions offer several advantages:

(a) the printing and processing system is dry and requires no chemicals
(b) printing may be done in ordinary lighting conditions
(c) the resultant image offers high resolution and is virtually grainless

100

Fig. 7.14. Metro/Kalver printer-processor for vesicular film

(though of course the stock cannot compensate for graininess in the original negative)

(d) the image is extremely stable and resistant to climatic and mechanical stresses

(e) printing and processing is quick and convenient (on specially designed machines).

Thermoplastic emulsions are normally coated on a support of transparent polyester which allows considerable saving in bulk over triacetate-based films, and the combination of base and emulsion provides an exceptionally durable, scratch resistant print film. The technique is limited, however, in that the print produced has a somewhat restricted density range, and is thus not entirely suitable for theatrical reproduction. Accordingly the system has been used so far principally for educational, industrial and scientific purposes and for the making of television prints from original cine negatives.

The Printer Characteristic

Printing inevitably involves a certain distortion of tonal values. A major factor is of course the D log E characteristic of the positive (or dupe negative) emulsion, but this can be distinguished from the characteristic of the printer itself. Ideally, the exposure of every area of the positive film would correspond exactly to the respective density of the negative, but because of the properties of the printer optical system areas of the positive image may in practice be relatively under- or over-exposed. The most significant item is

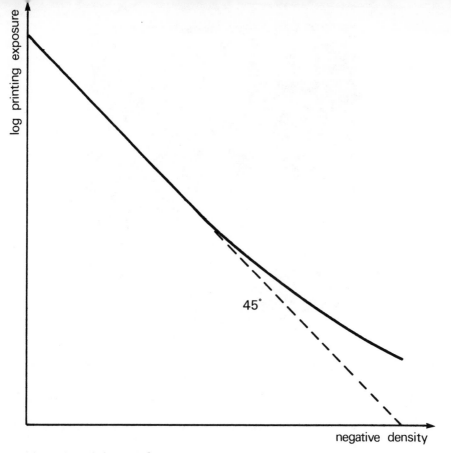

Fig. 7.15. *Optical printer flare curve*

flare, the effect of which may be illustrated by plotting negative density on a graph against log printing exposure (see Fig. 7.15). The 45° line represents a perfect transfer characteristic. It may be seen that the addition of flare illumination has the effect of lowering gamma particularly in areas of high negative density, which correspond to light tones in the subject. Printer flare is thus distinct from lens and camera flare and viewing flare, both of which have their major effect on dark areas in the subject.

Overall Transfer Characteristics

By constructing a chain of diagrams (frequently referred to as "quadrant" diagrams) illustrating the successive influences on the tone rendering of the subject of lens and camera flare, the negative characteristic, printer flare, the positive characteristic, projector flare, and viewing conditions, it is possible to trace the overall tone reproduction characteristic of the photographic system. (A more sophisticated analysis would of course take into account where necessary the characteristics of the duplicating positive and negative stocks and of the printer used for each additional step.) The results of such

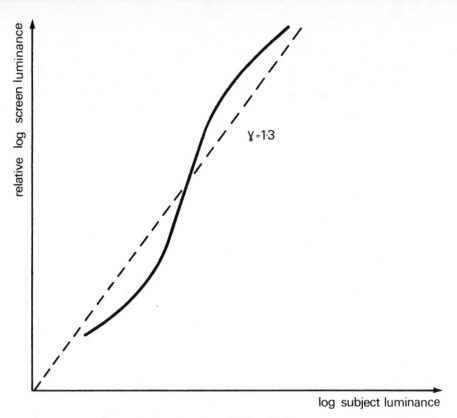

$\gamma=1\cdot3$

log subject luminance

Fig. 7.16. Overall reproduction curve for a black-and-white system

an investigation may be diagrammatically represented by a graph in which screen luminance in the cinema is compared with the luminance of the original subject (see Fig. 7.16).

The overall reproduction curve for a typical black-and-white motion picture system might resemble that illustrated. As can be seen, the major deviation from theoretical ideal transfer (dotted line)—apart from considerations of overall average gradient, discussed below—is the falling off of gamma at the light and dark ends of the luminance range. This means that, because of reduced contrast, the visibility of detail will be reduced in the highlights and deep shadow areas of the subject. In the middle range, on the other hand, the higher gamma results in slightly excessive tonal separation.

Overall gamma is the term used to describe the average contrastiness of the final release print when it is projected in standard viewing conditions. ("Gamma" is here used broadly to include all gradient measurements no matter how they are calculated.) As was mentioned in Chapter Five, an effective viewing gamma of approximately unity is required for naturalistic tonal rendering of the original scene, and there are several reasons why, for this condition to be fulfilled, the gamma of the final print (measured densitometrically) must be considerably higher than 1.0. Firstly, projector flare;

smoke, etc., in the auditorium, and stray light reflected from the screen all tend to reduce the effective contrast of the picture, and thus a projection factor is included in overall gamma calculations. Secondly, recent research indicates that viewing a film projected in a darkened room tends to lower the *apparent* gamma to the audience. This is because the darker the surround, the lighter the picture appears to be; but the effect is most marked in the shadow areas of the image. One recommendation is that the overall gamma for a film to be viewed with a dark surround should therefore be 1.5. In practice, however, black-and-white motion pictures tend to be made to an overall gamma of approximately 1.3, the figure being reached roughly in the following manner:

Original Scene		Camera and Lens Flare		Negative		Printer		Positive		Projection and Viewing Flare		Overall Gamma
1.0	x	0.9	x	0.65	x	0.95	x	2.6	x	0.9	=	1.3

If a duplicating stage is included the characteristics of the stocks used must be such that (allowing for printer flare)

$$\gamma \text{ FINE-GRAIN POSITIVE} \quad \text{x} \quad \gamma \text{ DUPE NEGATIVE} = 1$$

Overall gamma is higher in prints designed specifically for exhibition at drive-in theatres, to counteract excessive viewing flare, and in colour films.

A departure from the usual practice of developing projection prints to a standard gamma calculated from considerations of naturalistic tone rendering is involved in the recent introduction of variable contrast release positive stocks. The objective is to make available a choice of softer or harder prints which may be more appropriate, for aesthetic reasons, to the style and subject matter of the film. These stocks are particularly useful in colour photography, since alterations in gamma affect not only the contrast but also the colour saturation of the print, a subject which is considered in the following chapter.

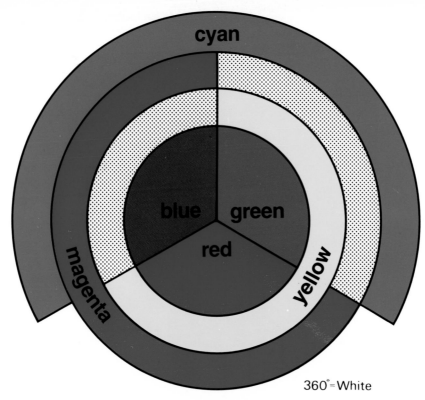

Fig. 8.1. A chromatic circle.

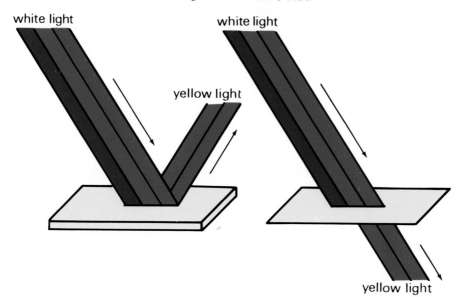

Fig. 8.2. Selective absorption: opaque coloured object and transparent coloured filter.

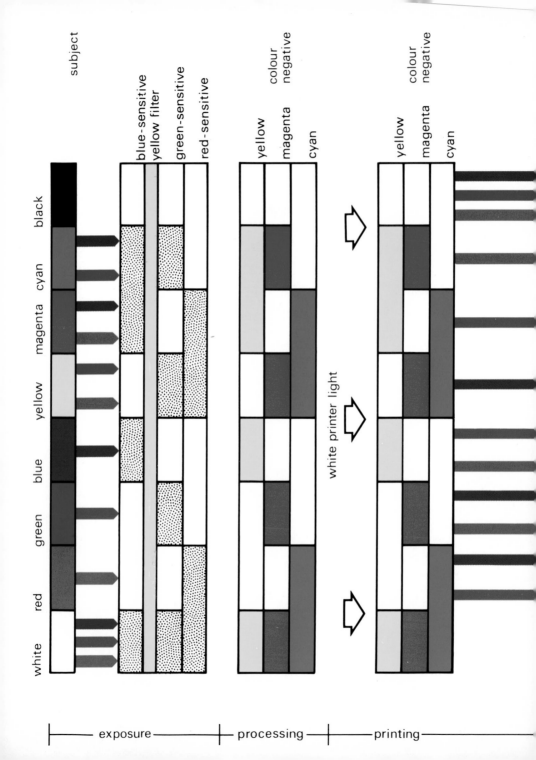

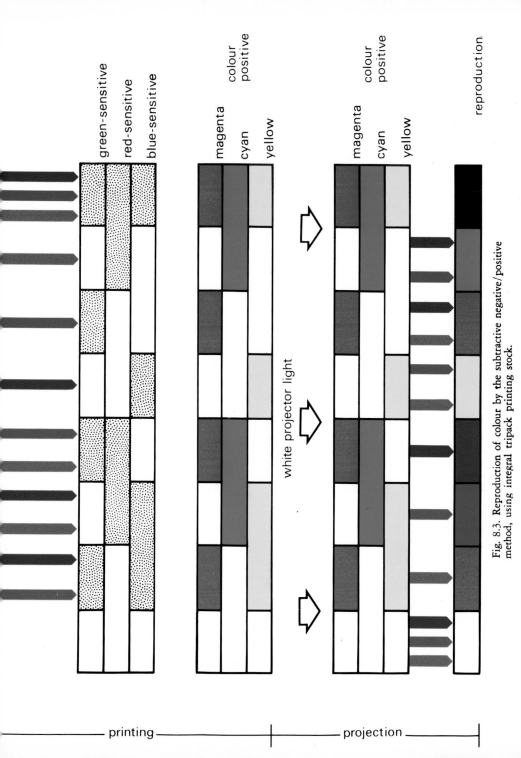

green-sensitive
red-sensitive
blue-sensitive

magenta
cyan
yellow
colour positive

white projector light

magenta
cyan
yellow
colour positive

reproduction

Fig. 8.3. Reproduction of colour by the subtractive negative/positive method, using integral tripack printing stock.

printing ——————— projection

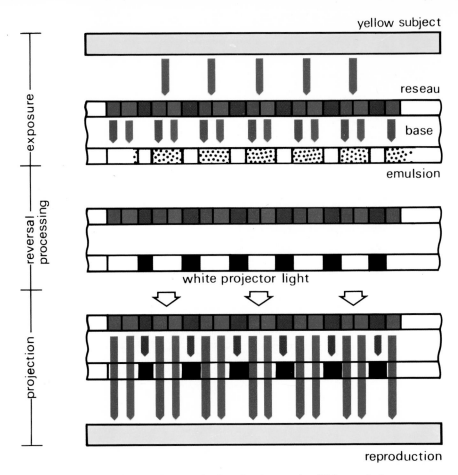

Fig. 8.4. Reproduction of colour by the mosaic additive method.

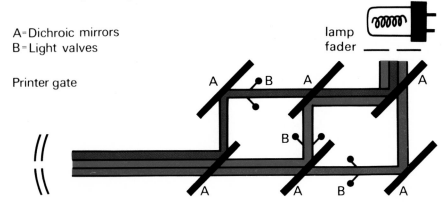

A = Dichroic mirrors
B = Light valves

Printer gate

lamp
fader

Fig. 8.5. Additive colour system as used in the Bell and Howell panel printer.

Chapter VIII
Introduction to Colour Photography

Most light sources, whether natural or artificial, are "white," i.e. they appear colourless and are composed of radiation from all parts of the visible spectrum in roughly equal proportions. They may be continuous or non-continuous in their spectral distribution (see Chapter One). The sensation of colour arises when light reaches the observer deficient in certain spectral regions. This occurs commonly if light from the source is transmitted through a medium which preferentially absorbs or refracts (blue sky, red lights), or is reflected from a selectively-absorbent surface (opaque coloured objects). In other cases, the source itself emits coloured light (fire, sodium lamps).

Because of the way the eye operates, discussed below, virtually every known colour may be produced by mixing three beams of light, from respectively the blue, green and red regions of the spectrum. BLUE, GREEN and RED, occupying approximately one-third of the spectrum each, are thus known as the *primary* colours (or *additive primaries,* since colours are created by adding the individual beams together, the mixture of all three producing white). There is a further set of three colours which are the *complements* of these, i.e. when mixed with them form white. Thus if blue is subtracted from white light, the resultant colour is yellow—a mixture of red and green. Magenta (red plus blue) is the complement of green, and "cyan" (blue plus green) the complement of red. YELLOW, MAGENTA and CYAN are known as the *secondary,* or *subtractive primary* colours and take up two-thirds of the spectrum each. The relationships may be illustrated by a diagram such as Fig. 8.1, in which the spectrum is represented in circular form with white light as 360°.

Such a diagram may usefully indicate the selective absorption, transmission and reflection characteristics of coloured objects and transparent filters. Objects reflect light of their own distinctive colour and absorb all other wavelengths, which if the illuminant is white combine to form the complementary colour. A magenta object, for example, absorbs green light. Similarly filters transmit (and reflect to a limited extent) light of their own colour and absorb complementary colours: thus yellow filters absorb blue light, while red filters absorb both blue and green (cyan).

The dominant wavelength of a colour determines its *hue,* or whether it is red, orange, yellow, etc. There are two further colour variables, *saturation* and *lightness.* Saturation is the extent to which the colour appears to be pure or free from admixture with white: thus vivid colours are highly saturated, and pale colours to a greater or lesser degree desaturated. Spectral colours, consisting of narrow adjoining bands of wavelengths, have 100% saturation, while grey, black and white have zero saturation. Lightness (also called *brightness*) is the relative quantity of light (of whatever wavelength) which the colour appears to emit. When light sources, as opposed to surfaces, are being referred to, the term employed is sometimes *luminosity.* These terms hue, saturation and lightness and luminosity are generally understood as being subjective: the objective equivalents are respectively *dominant wavelength, purity* and the photometric measures of luminance and luminous intensity.

The Trichromatic Theory of Vision

The mechanism of sight in human beings consists essentially (for each eye) of a lens to focus incoming rays of light into an image, a variable iris aperture to control the intensity of the light which is received, millions of light-sensitive elements distributed over the rear surface or retina of the eye, and a highly complex nerve system which transmits impulses from these receptors to the brain. The brain builds up from the signals which reach it a visual image comprising the various perceptions of lightness and darkness, colour, shape, movement, depth, texture and so on. The visual image so constructed differs in numerous ways from the type of image which is created by a photographic system: it is necessary to list here only a few of the more important:

(a) Human sight distinguishes *objects* whereas a photographic image registers patterns of light and shade or colours.

(b) Human sight is dynamic, the eye constantly darting and scanning the field of view, whereas even motion picture photography is by comparison static.

(c) The lens of the human eye forms an image which is sharply focussed only over a narrow angle at the centre of the visual field, the remainder of the image being fuzzy: a deficiency which is counteracted by frequent rapid eye movements. By comparison a photographic image formed by any regular lens is sharp over a very much wider angle.

(d) The field of view of the eye is indefinite, comprising a small area of sharp focus and a very much wider area of peripheral vision. Photographic images are normally abruptly delimited by a frame.

(e) Human eyesight is binocular, creating a three-dimensional impression which may be imitated photographically (with the exception of certain wide-angle effects) only by the employment of special stereoscopic systems.

(f) The conscious visual image constructed by the brain is noteworthy for the amount of information which is filtered out of it, as being either totally unnecessary or necessary only for unconscious processes such as orientation, balance, bodily movement etc. Photographic images are by comparison undiscriminating in the information they contain.

These considerations, of course, apply as well to monochrome as to colour photography. But since it is most often in the case of colour work that the "accuracy" or "realism" of the photographic rendering of a scene is brought into question, it is appropriate to include them here.

The photo-sensitive elements of the eye are of two basic kinds, known as "rods" and "cones." The rods are sensitive only to luminance levels and are concentrated towards the outer edge of the retina. *Scotopic vision,* as sight provided by the rods is termed, is particularly effective at lower levels of illumination. The cones are concentrated in a small central area of the retina (the "fovea centralis") and are able to distinguish colours. Cone or *photopic vision* is much more acute than rod vision but is operative only at relatively high illumination levels. The trichromatic theory of vision, for which evidence is steadily accumulating, states that there are three types of cones containing pigments whose chief absorptions lie roughly in the blue, green and red (or

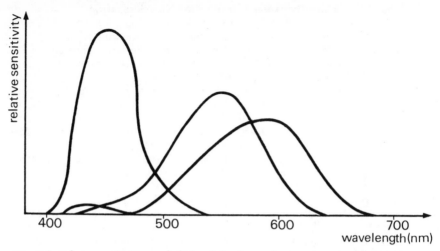

Fig. 8.6. Relative sensitivities to daylight of the three colour receptors in the eye

more precisely orange) segments of the spectrum respectively, and it is possible to construct speculative spectral sensitivity curves for each of the three types of receptor (see Fig. 8.6). As may be seen, the curves overlap. A colour is perceived, it is suggested, by an assessment in the brain of the relative response to the stimulant of the individual blue, green and red receptors, which are assumed to be distributed in mosaic fashion in roughly equal proportions. Thus if an observer has responses from the green and red receptors of virtually the same magnitude, but no response from the blue receptor, he sees yellow. It is the task of naturalistic colour photography to stimulate in reproduction the three types of cone in the same ratio as they were stimulated by the various areas of the original scene.

Colour Adaptation

The spectral sensitivity range of each receptor is believed to be constant under all lighting conditions, but the degree of response of one relative to the others may vary according to the colour temperature of the ambient light. This appears to be an automatic reaction derived from experience which ensures that within broad limits illumination appears colourless and surfaces which are known to be white do in fact look white. The process of adaptation may be observed when moving abruptly, for example, from an area of daylight to one of tungsten lighting. For a short period colours are seen as excessively yellowish, but a "normal" state is soon arrived at in which colours appear correct and virtually the same as under the former lighting conditions. Colour films—at least at their present stage of development—do not automatically adapt to the colour composition of the light source in this way. They are therefore "balanced" for light of a particular colour temperature, usually daylight or artificial light, and if exposed to the wrong light source without appropriate filter correction will produce pictures with a pronounced colour "cast" (see Chapter Eleven). Colour adaptation is one of a number of ways in which the nature of visual response complicates the reproduction of colour, and is examined more fully later.

The Relationship between Illumination and Saturation

The basic factors affecting the saturation of colours are (a) the absolute intensity of illumination and (b) the extent to which illumination is specular or diffuse. The theory of rod and cone vision adequately explains the first. Below a level of about ½ foot-candle the cones, on which colour vision is dependent, are completely inoperative, and thus colours at night (without artificial illumination) are desaturated to the point of being non-existent. Above light levels of ½ foot-candle the cones begin to come into play, accounting for a little at first and then an ever-increasing proportion of total vision. Saturation increases as the colour-insensitive rods are gradually displaced as the dominant light receptors, until at higher levels of illumination the cones take over completely. Thus in brilliant lighting, such as tropical sunshine which may reach levels of 12,000 to 15,000 foot-candles, saturation is extremely high and colours very vivid. The second factor was touched upon in Chapter One. Any partial reflector, and most coloured surfaces are of this type, mixes specular (white) and diffuse (coloured) reflection from an ordinary white light source. If the illumination itself is diffuse, specularly reflected white light will be bounced off in all directions and will inevitably desaturate the colour of the object, no matter what the position of the observer. If however the illumination is specular, or strongly directional, specularly reflected rays will be limited to a single angle and the observer viewing the object from a direction other than this will receive a high proportion of diffuse reflection. Saturation thus increases as the ratio of specular to diffuse lighting of the subject is raised.

It is an important consideration in colour photography that the influence of the first of these factors results from the physiological structure of the eye and is not operative at all in the case of photographic emulsions. Colour films, that is, which are correctly exposed will record virtually no difference in the saturation of a coloured surface whether the illumination is tropical sunshine or moonlight. It is for this reason that colour photographs taken in gloomy lighting conditions may be—by comparison with the visual appearance of the original subject—surprisingly vivid, and it is often a deliberate policy to exploit this effect in lighting for motion pictures.

Additive Methods of Colour Photography

Colour photography exploits the trichromatic principle of vision by breaking down each area of the scene to be reproduced into its components of blue, green and red light and recording them separately. There then exist several methods by which the independent records may be processed and re-combined to form an acceptable colour reproduction of the original scene.

The simplest and earliest forms of colour photography were based on the *additive* principle. According to this, all colours may be reproduced by projecting on the screen independent beams of blue, green and red light. Where the three overlap, white is produced. The procedure then is to photograph the scene independently through blue, green and red filters. If the separate positive black-and-white transparencies so derived are then projected on to a screen in register, through filters of the same colour as used when photographing, the colours of the original scene will be reconstructed. A red area in the original, for example, will be recorded as a low density in the positive red record, but as high densities in the other transparencies, since red light is absorbed by blue and green filters. The only light reaching the screen in

screen

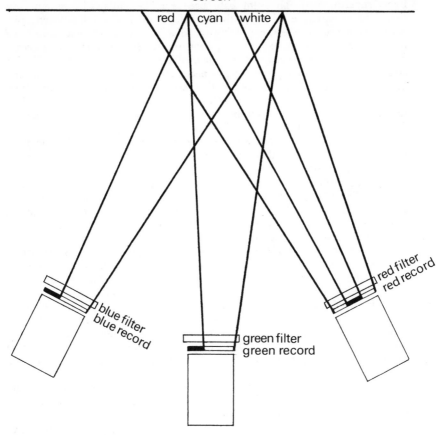

red cyan white

blue filter
blue record

green filter
green record

red filter
red record

Fig. 8.7. Reproduction of colours by the triple-projector additive method

the area of the image representing the red part of the original therefore will be that transmitted through the red filter. A bluish green or cyan portion of the original would expose areas of both the blue and green records, and would accordingly be reproduced by a mixture of blue and green light in projection, while white, of course, would be recorded on every transparency and be reproduced by the superimposition of all three primaries (see Fig. 8.7).

The triple projector technique could not be used for motion picture photography because of the problems posed by registration and synchronisation requirements. Accordingly various ingenious methods were devised whereby the additive principle could be employed with only a single projector. These are now essentially of historical interest, but it is worthwhile to examine two such methods—the Dufaycolor technique and the Technicolor two-strip additive process—as an indication of the possibilities available.

The Dufaycolor system, like other "mosaic" methods, was based on the pointilliste principle that adjacent dots of primary colours, provided they are sufficiently small with respect to the viewer, may appear to merge to form other colours almost as if pigments were mixed in solution or coloured

109

lights superimposed. The film base used for the Dufaycolor system was coated on the opposite side from the emulsion with a very fine geometrically-patterned screen or reseau consisting of adjacent patches of blue, green and red dyes. With a single exposure through the screen and film base, separate colour records were obtained in fragmented form on the same piece of film, and hence only a single projector was necessary. Reversal processing was employed, and the mosaic of coloured patches resulting from shining light through the film with its reseau still intact gave reasonably good colour reproduction. Yellow, for example, was represented by this method by adjacent patches of red and green light rather than, as in the triple-projector technique, superimposed red and green beams (see Fig. 8.4). Dufaycolor was a reasonably successful commercial colour process which continued to be used into the Fifties.

The Technicolor two-strip additive method was used between 1917 and 1922. Unlike Dufaycolor, it maintained the principle of using purely black-and-white film, colour being introduced by means of filters on the projector. The basis of the method was a specially-designed camera which divided the light entering through the single lens into two parts by means of a beam-splitting prism. By a combination of filters and appropriate dye sensitisation of the emulsions, two negative records were obtained simultaneously, the first of the yellow-red and the second of the blue-green components of the exposing light. After processing and printing, the two colour records were combined in the theatre by projecting them through separate apertures with red and green filters, the two images being brought into register by dint of a special attachment which according to contemporary accounts necessitated a somewhat acrobatic projectionist. The system demonstrated that some kind of colour rendering could be obtained by an ultra-simple division of the spectrum into two regions, and in fact two-colour systems were to survive long beyond the demise of the additive Technicolor method. However there were, of course, inherent deficiencies, the most obvious being that reds became too orange and blues too greenish.

Additive methods have been completely superseded by the alternative subtractive techniques in the motion picture industry, but they survive in colour television, which is a modern application of the mosaic principle. Miniature triads of fluorescent phosphors coated on to the inner face of the cathode ray tube emit appropriate intensities of blue, green and red light when electronically stimulated. The use of coloured phosphors avoids one of the major deficiencies of the usual additive methods, heavy light absorption (see below).

Disadvantages of Additive Methods

The basic disadvantages of additive methods are:

(a) *Heavy light absorption.* For correct colour rendition, the filters used for additive reproduction must be saturated, so that, for example, the red filter will absorb all light from the blue and green regions of the spectrum. Theoretically, this means that the filters used in a tri-colour system will have a transmission factor of 33%, but the absorption characteristics of dyes are such that in practice the figure is more like 20%. As a result, the highest intensity on the screen, a brilliant white, will utilise only one-fifth of the light from the projector or projectors. Any other image area, whether grey or coloured, will involve further absorption from silver deposits in the developed emulsion. A fully saturated red, for example, is rendered in the mosaic additive system by about 20% of the light falling on one-third of the colour elements, or less than 7% of the total light used for projection. Such heavy light absorption necessitates the use of high wattage projection lamps and hence elaborate cooling systems, and incidentally makes it impossible to produce reflection colour prints by additive methods.

(b) *Loss of picture definition (mosaic techniques).* The colour elements used in building up the image by mosaic methods are of necessity larger than the silver grains. There is consequently a loss of definition and the mosaic pattern becomes obtrusive with only a small degree of enlargement.

(c) *Limitations in colour rendering and need for special projection equipment (two-strip additive techniques).* Because of the complications in projection, systems such as the early Technicolor method described are restricted to a two-colour reproductive process whose limitations have been pointed out. Moreover the need for special projection equipment and for highly skilled operators to achieve even roughly accurate registration of the separate images limits the usefulness of this type of additive method still further.

These disadvantages count heavily against additive techniques and all modern colour film processes utilise the subtractive principle, discussed in the next chapter.

Chapter IX
Colour Photography:
The Subtractive Principle

In the additive system, colours are formed by superimposing or juxtaposing, in the appropriate proportions, patches of blue, green and red light from separate sources. Yellow, for example, is obtained by mixing red and green: from the beams of two projectors, for instance, or from adjacent sections, independently filtered, of a single projector beam. There is, however, a second way of producing colours.

Consideration of a chromatic circle (Fig. 8.1) reveals not only that RED + GREEN = YELLOW, but also that YELLOW + BLUE = WHITE. Yellow, in other words, may be formed by *subtracting blue* from a white light source, that is by placing a yellow (blue-absorbing) filter over the projector beam. Subtractive systems in fact employ three dyes—of the secondary colours —which operate as filters controlling independently the absorption of the three primaries:

$$\begin{array}{lll} \text{CYAN} & \text{subtracts} & \text{RED} \\ \text{MAGENTA} & \text{subtracts} & \text{GREEN} \\ \text{YELLOW} & \text{subtracts} & \text{BLUE.} \end{array}$$

Since, as we have seen, virtually all colours may be reproduced by varying the relative proportions of the three primaries red, green and blue, the subtractive system like the additive provides a workable basis for colour photography.

The great advantage of the subtractive method is that the dyes used may be superimposed over a single light beam. This is because each filter absorbs up to roughly *one-third* of the total spectrum, and it requires the superimposition of all three dyes at full concentration to reduce the white light beam to black. Additive filters, by contrast, absorb up to *two-thirds* of the spectrum each, and any two filters placed over each other result in zero transmission: superimposed red and green filters, for example, produce not yellow but black. Subtractive methods thus obviate the need for complicated projector equipment and do not suffer from the lack of definition and obtrusive colour patch patterns characteristic of mosaic systems.

A second major advantage of the smaller absorption range of subtractive dyes is the much higher efficiency which results. We may compare, for example, the rendition of white, a secondary colour and a primary colour (both saturated) by the two systems, assuming ideal dye absorption characteristics:

	Additive	% of total projection light (ideal)	*Subtractive*	% of total projection light (ideal)
WHITE	red+blue+green	33	clear transparency	100
YELLOW	red+green	22	white—blue	66
RED	red	11	white—blue—green	33

This factor assumes even greater importance when the practical absorption characteristics of dyes are taken into account (see Chapter Eight).

A further advantage of the subtractive system is that virtually any colour at any luminance level (within the normal limitations of projection) may be reproduced simply by superimposition of dyes. A silver image is thus no longer necessary in the projection print.

Absorption Characteristics of Subtractive Colour Dyes

The yellow, magenta and cyan dyes used in subtractive colour reproduction should each control roughly one-third of the spectrum. The precise optimum points at which lines should be drawn between the blue, green and red regions is open to argument, but there is a good deal of agreement on the current convention, which is:

BLUE:		→ 490nm
GREEN:	490nm	→ 580nm
RED:	580nm	→

It is clear that any trichromatic method of colour reproduction, whether additive or subtractive, which divides the spectrum into three distinct regions like this is incapable of distinguishing between two pure spectral colours lying within the same band, which the eye can do because the sensitivity curves of the colour receptors overlap. Thus two spectral hues of the same intensity lying within the "red" region, say an orange of 600nm and a pure red of 650nm, are virtually indistinguishable in a trichromatic reproduction. Fortunately, however, coloured objects normally reflect light in varying proportions from most regions of the spectrum, and are thus registered on each colour record. Accurate distinction of hue is therefore possible in the great majority of cases.

Ideally, the dyes employed should delimit their absorption regions sharply, so that their spectral absorption curves for various degrees of concentration should be those indicated by the straight lines in Fig. 9.1. If this could be achieved, light would be absorbed at any wavelength by one and only one of the dyes, the others having 100% transmission. If, instead, the curves overlapped, as has sometimes been suggested, so that they approximated more closely the spectral sensitivity curves of the eye, any gain in accuracy of hue rendition would be more than counterbalanced by the decrease in luminosity resulting from heavier light absorption. If on the other hand the absorption bands were narrower, and thus not contiguous, there would be certain wavelengths at which no absorption took place and black could therefore not be formed.

The curved lines in Fig. 9.1 indicate the absorption characteristics of a set of practical subtractive dyes. It may be seen that the magenta and cyan dyes both have significant unwanted absorptions, the magenta in the blue region, and the cyan in both blue and green. The result of this is that blues and greens tend to be reproduced darker than they should be unless corrective measures are taken. Fortunately there exist techniques of *masking,* and in particular the cunning device of *coloured couplers,* described in the next chapter, by which this problem may be overcome.

Since coloured objects normally reflect light from most regions of the spectrum to some degree, all three dyes are usually present over most areas of the image. It is only in the case of very light or very saturated colours

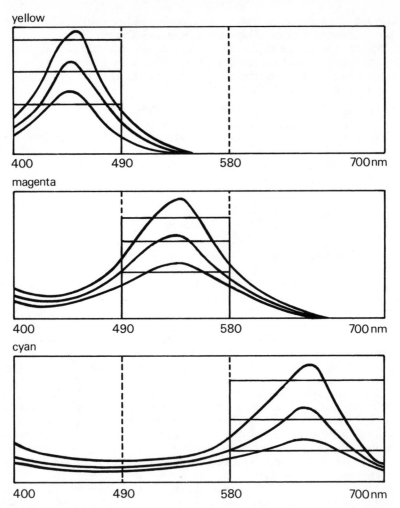

Fig. 9.1. Ideal and practical absorption characteristics of a set of subtractive dyes, at various concentrations

that the concentration of a particular dye may be reduced to zero. There is thus a general absorption throughout the spectrum which represents a basic grey level, the density of which determines the lightness or darkness of the image, and to which appropriate quantities of dye may be regarded as being added to form the relevant colours.

The reproduction of greys is one of the most crucial tests of a colour photographic process, since it requires equal absorptions by the right concentrations of dye in all three regions of the spectrum. An imbalance will result in colour bias, with the greys tinted yellow, magenta or cyan or some combination of these, and the colour rendering of the complete picture affected equivalently. An accurate colour process should reproduce a grey scale as grey over a complete range of tones from black to white.

114

The Integral Tripack

The discussion up to this point has been concerned with examining how colours may be reproduced by superimposing a set of subtractive dyes and placing them in the beam of a white projector lamp, assuming that it was possible by some photographic means to locate the dyes on the transparent support in the correct areas and concentrations for the accurate reproduction of the original scene. It is next necessary to consider how this may be achieved.

The first necessity, as with additive colour methods, is to obtain separate colour records using regular silver halide emulsions of the blue, green and red components of the scene. An early and widespread method of doing this was by means of the three-strip Technicolor camera, which incorporated a beam-splitting prism behind a specially-designed taking lens. The three records were made on separate negative films by the use of appropriate filters and sensitisation of the emulsions, two of the films being run in bipack, i.e. in contact with each other.

Since the Technicolor camera was bulky and cumbersome, attempts were made to attach the three emulsions to a single film base. The earliest versions along these lines had the emulsions manufactured as skins which could be stripped off separately and secured to individual supports. This, however, required relatively thick emulsion layers with the result that blurring of the image through irradiation was a serious problem. The real breakthrough only came when methods were devised whereby the three emulsion layers could be distinguished during processing to produce independent dye images without being separated from the film base. Success in the commercial development of these techniques led to the establishment of the *integral tripack*, which has now supplanted virtually every other type of colour film.

As with the films used in the Technicolor camera, the principle of dye sensitisation of emulsions (see Chapter One) is exploited. This method minimises the use of filters and hence of light loss. The conventional layout of tripack colour stock, the arrangement which has been found most satisfactory in practice, is shown in cross-section in Fig. 9.2. The top layer, which is not colour-sensitised, registers only blue light. Below this is a yellow filter layer which absorbs any further blue light not already absorbed by the halide grains in the top layer. The second emulsion is orthochromatic, i.e. not sensitive to red. Since all the blue light from the subject is already absorbed by the top layer or the filter interposed beneath it, this emulsion records only the green component of the scene. The remaining light, from the red region of the spectrum, is recorded on the bottom emulsion which is panchromatic but designed to have low spectral sensitivity to green. In some tripack materials an anti-halation layer is inserted beneath the red-sensitive emulsion, instead of being coated to the underside of the base in the normal fashion.

Creation of Dye Images

The independent silver images carrying the separate blue, green and red records must now be converted to positive dye images of the appropriate colour, as follows:

BLUE record (top emulsion layer)   → YELLOW positive dye image
GREEN record (middle emulsion layer) → MAGENTA positive dye image
RED record (bottom emulsion layer)   →   CYAN positive dye image

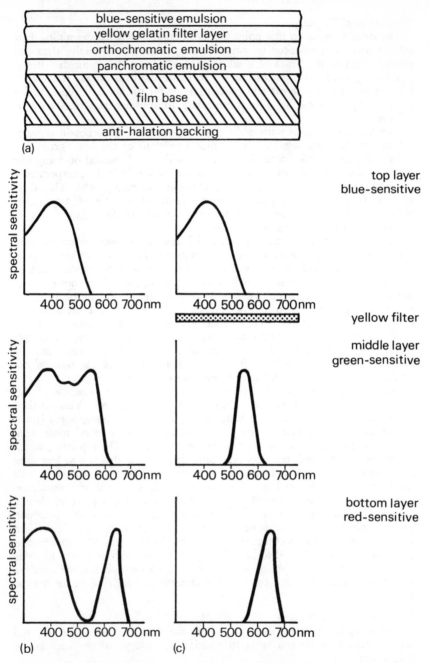

Fig. 9.2. *The integral tripack: (a) cross-section of the emulsion layers (b) spectral sensitivity of each emulsion (c) effective spectral sensitivity of each emulsion after filtration*

The conversion may be direct, via reversal processing, or indirect following a negative/positive system. The dye images of the projection print are positive in the sense that dye concentrations are at a maximum in those areas of the picture where density would be highest in a positive black-and-white silver image. Thus the lightest and most saturated blue, for example, would be represented by the *minimum* concentration of yellow dye.

There are several methods by which this conversion may be carried out, but all involve a process of *colour development.* This technique, which is described in more detail in the following chapter, requires the use of *couplers* which by reacting with the oxidised developer products form dye globules of the correct colour around the exposed emulsion grains:

$$\text{oxidised developer} + \text{coupler} \rightarrow \text{insoluble dye.}$$

In certain processes for producing still transparencies, the couplers are added to the developing solutions, but in motion picture practice the couplers are incorporated during manufacture in the emulsion layers.

Giving colour development to the grains originally exposed results, after bleaching of the metallic silver and fixing to remove residual halides, in a *colour negative.* The dyes making up the image are (generally, but not necessarily) the familiar subtractive ones of yellow, magenta and cyan in the top, middle and bottom layers respectively, but the concentrations are the opposite of those which will be necessary in the final projection print. Thus, in the negative stage, a very light, saturated blue would be recorded by the *maximum* concentration of yellow dye. Consequently in a colour negative colours appear complementary in addition to tonalities being reversed.

From a colour negative, release prints may be produced either by printing through on to tripack stock similar in principle to the original camera film (usually via one or more intermediate stages), or by a *dye imbibition* process, such as Technicolor. Alternatively, the camera film may be designed for reversal processing. In this case a positive dye image is obtained on the same film base as that on which the original exposure was made.

Colour Densitometry

The densitometry of colour materials presents some special problems. Since black-and-white silver images are to a large extent non-selective in their absorption characteristics—in other words density remains very nearly constant throughout the visible spectrum—the colour temperature of the light source and the relative spectral sensitivity of the light detector used in the densitometer are fairly unimportant. This is not so in colour. Here it is necessary to ascertain the density of an image which is made up by the superimposition of three dye layers having their chief absorptions in different regions of the spectrum. The combined density of the three dyes is by no means constant at all wavelengths (see Fig. 9.3). Moreover, it is necessary to obtain density readings from different parts of the spectrum in order to study the colour balance of the image.

The method by which this is done normally is to insert in the light beam a set of three filters in succession, which enable readings to be taken separately of the density of the film to blue, green and red light. It is important to recognize that the results obtained from colour densitometry depend to a very great extent upon the particular set of filters used, and they must therefore be chosen with some care for the specific task in hand.

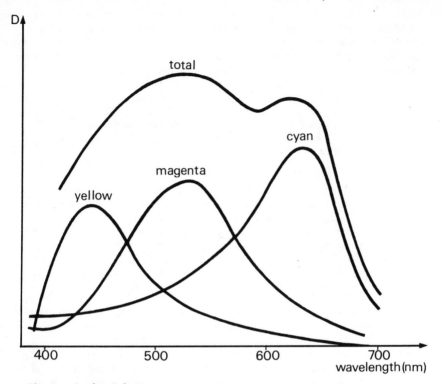

Fig. 9.3. Combined density of a set of three subtractive dyes

An initial design consideration is that only visible light should be registered by the light detector. For this reason it is usually necessary to incorporate a dichroic filter of such characteristics that it cuts off transmission from the lamp sharply at the 700nm end of the spectrum. Infra-red radiation may in addition be attenuated by a heat-absorbing glass inserted in the light path to prevent over-heating of the film or filter.

The wide variety of filters used in colour densitometry may be grouped into two basic classes, according as to whether they are intended for measuring *integral density* or *analytical density*. The distinction is necessary because the spectral absorption curves of the dye sets used in tripack materials overlap. Thus the density of the sample at any given wavelength or waveband is composed of the individual densities of all three dyes. Integral density is a measure of the *total* absorption of the dyes in combination, while analytical density (which can often be calculated algebraically) refers to the absorption of the yellow, magenta or cyan dyes alone.

For normal quality control in motion picture work integral density measurements are found to be satisfactory. Filters are chosen according to the nature of the film being tested. For films which are to be projected, whether colour prints or reversal originals, a set of three narrow-cut filters with arbitrarily selected spectral transmission bands may be employed, provided that standardisation is achieved by restricting comparative results to a single set

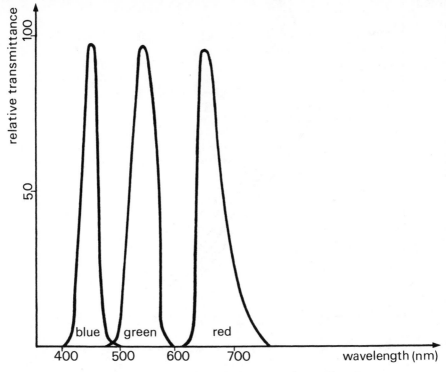

Fig. 9.4. Spectral transmittances of a set of three printing density filters

of image dyes. For "pre-print" films—colour negatives, intermediates, internegatives and reversal originals which are to be printed—a particular variety of integral densities known as *printing densities* are measured. The filters for this purpose are designed to reproduce the emulsion layer sensitivities of the colour print film to be used, in combination with a specific type of printer, as well as taking into account the relative spectral sensitivity of the light receptor incorporated in the densitometer. Spectral transmittance curves of a typical set of printing density filters are illustrated in Fig. 9.4.

Colour Film Characteristics

Plotting integral (or printing) densities against log exposure with a colour film results in a set of three characteristic curves referring to the absorption by the image dyes of blue, green and red light respectively. In general terms, a scene will be reproduced without colour bias if the three curves are coincident. However there are many factors to be taken into account here. Thus in the characteristic illustrated (Fig. 9.5), which is for a reversal original stock suitable for projection, the red curve lies above and to the right of the green curve, which is similarly spaced from the curve indicating density to blue. The reason for this is basically that this type of film is designed for projection by tungsten light, which is yellowish in colour: this may be compensated for by slightly increasing the speed of the film with respect to blue light, and decreasing it with respect to red.

119

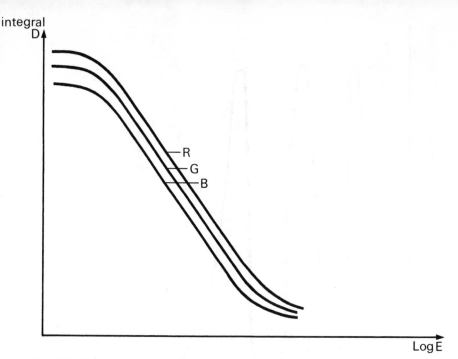

integral D (vertical axis)

R
G
B

LogE (horizontal axis)

Fig. 9.5. Characteristic of a colour reversal original film suitable for projection

If in a particular case the curves do not coincide as they are designed to, they are said to be *mis-matched*. Exposing a colour film to light of a different colour temperature from that to which it is balanced (see Chapter Eleven), for example, results in horizontal displacement which indicates a shift in the relative speeds of the emulsion layers. Provided that the shift is relatively small, it may be compensated for in printing. Such adjustments are facilitated if the camera film has a long straight-line characteristic.

Printing corrections cannot however be readily made for mis-matched slope and curvature in the film characteristic. Thus an important requirement of tripack stocks is that the three emulsions attain the same gamma with one development time. Again, it is desirable that exposure and processing result in curves having identical toe portions.

As mentioned above, colour characteristic curves depend very greatly on the set of filters with which measurements are taken, which in turn depend on the printer-film combination, etc., which a particular laboratory employs. In the absence of complete information they can therefore be misleading, and it is not usually the practice of film stock manufacturers to publish colour characteristics in their film specification leaflets.

The basic properties of the various types of colour film stock are as follows: (a) *Colour negative* stocks generally incorporate coloured couplers for the purpose of masking (see Chapter Ten). The recommended gamma is approximately 0.65 as for monochrome negative materials, but the maximum density attained by the dye image is somewhat lower than the densities reached in black-and-white negatives.

(b) *Colour intermediate* (positive or negative) stocks are used for duplicate printing. Coloured couplers are again employed. Gamma closely approximates 1.0 so that no alteration in tonal rendering takes place at any stage during the duplication process, the same stock being used to produce both master positives and dupe negatives.

(c) *Colour reversal intermediate* films have been recently introduced to telescope the two intermediate phases necessary when printing with regular negative/positive stocks and development techniques, thereby improving colour quality and definition. Gamma is 1.0 so that accurate duplicate negatives are produced directly from the original camera film.

(d) *Colour print* films are designed for release printing from a variety of pre-print materials. The location of the curves with respect to each other is calculated to minimise the filter adjustments necessary in making prints for various types of projection light, etc., given the models of printer commonly in use in the industry. For theatrical release, recommended gamma is in the range 2.4 to 3.0, thus ensuring high contrast reproduction (see below).

(e) *Colour reversal original* stocks fall into two classes. The first, intended primarily as a pre-print film, has a comparatively low contrast, being designed to be developed to a gamma of about 1.0. The characteristic curves are usually fairly straight, facilitating matching when the original is printed on to an internegative or directly on to a reversal print stock. The second class consists of reversal stocks which are suitable for direct projection, though they may also be printed if necessary. Gamma is approximately 1.4, and the speed of some stocks of this category is considerably higher than that of other colour films currently available. Neither type of reversal original normally incorporates coloured couplers for masking.

(f) *Colour internegative* films are used when an intermediate stage is desired in the printing of reversal originals. One advantage of the extra stage is that internegative films in general have coloured couplers for masking purposes and thus better colour reproduction in the final print is possible. So that the contrast of the image in the projection print is equivalent to that produced by other procedures, the gamma of internegative films is around 0.65.

(g) *Colour reversal print* stocks, as the name indicates, enable release copies to be printed directly from a reversal original, normally of the second type above. Depending on the process, films of this category have approximately unit contrast so that the tone rendering of the original is not altered.

There are also special colour print materials for television transmission (see Chapter Twelve).

Particularly with colour films, high quality results can only be attained if the processing and printing procedures specified by the manufacturers are closely adhered to. When a new stock introduced to the market requires a special process, the details of this, formulas and so on, will be published by the manufacturer.

Contrast in Colour Films

In general a very contrasty subject does not reproduce well in colour. This is not necessarily because colour films have less latitude than black-and-white stocks, although this is true in some cases, but because of a variety of other factors.

The most important of these is that, in order to counteract losses in saturation during reproduction, professional colour film systems are designed for a final high contrast print which will be satisfactory in quality only if the lighting of the original subject is comparatively flat. In practice a lighting contrast ratio not exceeding 4:1 is recommended to achieve best results in a system which may produce an overall gamma as high as 1.6, as compared with a typical black-and-white figure of 1.3.

A second consideration is that of shadow illumination. Unless shadows are lit with sufficient fill light—which reduces the lighting contrast—they tend not to be reproduced as their own colour or as neutral greys or blacks, but instead take on a colour which is predominant in the scene or which is reflected into the shadow area from a nearby object. In many cases this is in fact the true colour of the light coming from this area of the subject, but it is not seen as such because of compensating mechanisms in the human eye.

Flat lighting is acceptable in colour photography because to a large extent tonal separation is provided by colour contrast, and it is unnecessary to attempt further differentiation of subject areas by boosting contrast in lighting. If the film is shot specifically for television transmission, it is desirable to restrict the lighting contrast ratio even more (see Chapter Twelve).

Chapter X
Processing and Printing Colour Film

Colour Development

The basis of colour development is the fact that a group of organic chemicals known as couplers will react with the development products of some developing agents, notably paraphenylenediamine and its derivatives, to form insoluble dyes of the hues required for subtractive colour reproduction, the process taking place simultaneously with the reduction of the exposed halide grains to metallic silver. The colour of the dye formed depends upon the constitution of the coupler, and thus independent yellow, magenta and cyan images may be formed in separate layers during a single development process by the incorporation of the appropriate couplers in the emulsion coatings during manufacture.

The amount of dye formed at any one spot in the image is dependent upon the quantity of oxidised developer liberated by the reduction process, which in turn depends on the intensity of exposure at that point. Dye globules will therefore be formed in greater concentrations in the areas of heavier exposure and hence higher density in the developed image. It should be noted that the dyes are formed around the silver grains, and thus while a dye image after bleaching is technically grainless, the grain structure of the emulsion is in fact reproduced by a degree of blurring and by minute variations in dye concentration over constant density areas.

As was mentioned in Chapter Three, the concentration of sulphite as a preservative in the solution must be kept low in order to prevent its competing with the couplers for the oxidised developing agent, and thus reducing dye yield. The consequent danger of aerial oxidation may be reduced by the addition of other anti-oxidants to the solution, but sulphite cannot be entirely eliminated.

Colour development is a crucial stage in the colour reproduction process, since many factors must be regulated within close limits if correct colour rendering is to be achieved. An important consideration is that the rate of development and coupling should be as equal as possible in the three layers, so that the contrast obtained is similar for the blue, green and red records. This requires accurate analysis and regulation of the constitution of the colour developing agent. A complicating factor is the possibility of the oxidised developer migrating to an adjacent layer before reacting with couplers ("proximity development").

The three silver images are normally removed by means of a rehalogenising bleach which reconverts the silver to halides, which are then dissolved out along with the unexposed halides in the fixing solution. Generally the yellow filter layer also vanishes during bleaching. The unused coupler molecules do not impair the definition or colour rendering of the image and are therefore allowed to remain: in the case of coloured couplers (see below) their effect is in fact beneficial.

Virtually all available motion picture colour negative and reversal film stocks have dye couplers which are incorporated in the emulsion layers during manufacture. Historically, the two most serious difficulties encountered in producing couplers for the purpose of colour development were the problem of finding substances which would be compatible with silver halides and gelatin, and the task of preventing the couplers from wandering by diffusion from their appointed layers. The first was overcome with the discovery of the organic agents (notably phenolic derivatives and compounds containing a reactive methylene group) now in use. The second problem was surmounted in several ways, as for example by attaching a long, heavy, inert molecular chain to each molecule of coupler, as first employed by Agfa, or by dissolving the couplers in an oily solvent and dispersing them throughout the emulsion in the form of tiny droplets approximately one-tenth the size of halide grains, a technique first used by the Eastman Kodak Company. Another possible method is combining the coupler with the gelatin in such a way that vertical diffusion is prevented.

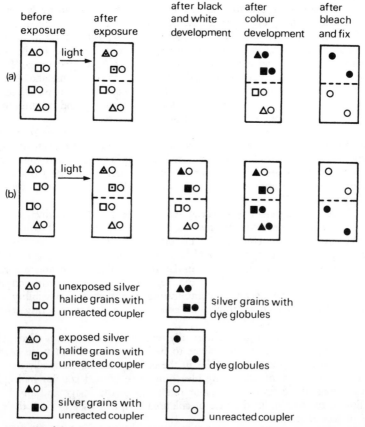

Fig. 10.1. *Simplified representation of the formation of a dye image in one of the layers of an integral tripack, by (a) colour negative and (b) colour reversal process*

The following is a typical basic processing sequence for a colour negative film:

1. Colour development
2. Bleaching
3. Fixing
4. Washing
5. Drying.

Intermediate washing and separate stages to remove the anti-halation backing, etc., may also be required.

Motion picture colour reversal film for professional purposes is mainly used at present as a camera stock only in 16mm, in which gauge it is also used for the production of release prints from reversal originals or from 35mm colour positives. In 35mm colour reversal stock is employed as an intermediate film for the production of dupe negatives directly from the original colour negative.

The principle of developing reversal film with couplers incorporated in the emulsion layers is that after initial (black-and-white) development of the film, a latent image must be created in the halide grains not exposed to light on the original exposure. This may be done either by exposing the film uniformly on both sides to white light, or by using a "fogging" colour developing agent, i.e. one which does not distinguish between exposed and unexposed halide grains. In practice the second method is now much the more common. The latent image is converted to positive dye images in each of the three layers by colour development in the normal way. The fundamental processing sequence is:

1. Black-and-white development
2. Washing
3. Drying
4. Colour development (with fogging agent)
5. Bleaching
6. Fixing
7. Washing
8. Drying.

Bleaching and fixing are sometimes combined in a single operation. Other stages which may be incorporated in the processing sequence include intermediate washing and drying, stop baths, and special treatment of the sound track in the case of printing stock.

Dyes Used in Colour Negative Materials

It is customary in colour negatives to employ the same subtractive dyes, in the same layers, as those used for the positive print, with the result that all colours are reproduced as their complementary hue. This is not, however, essential for correct colour reproduction by the negative/positive process. The only requisite is that in printing, the dyes should be able to isolate the superimposed blue, green and red records of the original scene so that they are represented in the positive by yellow, magenta and cyan images respectively. For this purpose it would be perfectly acceptable if in the negative the blue record was developed to form a cyan image, and so on, provided only that distinct dyes were used in each layer. This would merely require a tripack printing stock in which the combination of dye couplers and selectively sensitised emulsions had been appropriately adjusted. In the alternative imbibition printing process variations in the dye layer structure of the negative could be easily accommodated by a simple switch in the choice of dyes for each matrix.

Masking with Coloured Couplers

Masking is a method of correcting for the unwanted absorptions of the three subtractive colour dyes (see Chapter Nine). A simple, effective and automatic means of masking is the employment of dye couplers which are themselves coloured.

Consider, for example, the undesired absorption by magenta dyes of light in the blue region of the spectrum. If uncorrected, this results in blues which are too dark and yellows which are too light. Moreover, any colours incorporating some percentage of blue will be off balance: magenta, for example, will be too reddish. Now if the magenta dye used was at a constant concentration throughout the image, the unwanted blue absorption could be counteracted by increasing the blue content of the light used for printing, which may be done very simply. But the problem in normal colour photography is that the concentrations of any particular dye are varied over the whole image area. Therefore in the case of the magenta dye, for example, it is necessary to find a method of correcting for relatively high excess blue absorption in areas where the magenta dye is heavily concentrated, and low unwanted absorptions in low concentration areas.

The idea of coloured couplers arises from the consideration that the concentration of dye over any small image area is inversely proportional to the amount of residual unused coupler at that spot. If the dye is at 100% concentration, for example, all the available coupler will have been used up by reaction with liberated development products. Conversely, in an area of low dye concentration the proportion of remaining unreacted coupler is naturally high.

Suppose, then, that the coupler used in the magenta-forming layer is designed to absorb blue light, i.e. coloured yellow. The residual amounts of unused coupler may then be employed to cancel out, approximately, the variations in blue absorption caused by the uneven concentrations of magenta dye. This is illustrated in Fig. 10.2. Let us assume that at full concentration the magenta dye has a 50% absorption of blue, in addition to its regular absorption of green. In such areas there will be no residual coupler and the dye will thus be responsible for the total blue absorption of the layer. At the other extreme, in parts of the image where the concentration of magenta dye is zero, blue light will be absorbed only by the residual coupler, the amount of which will here be at a maximum. The colour of the coupler may be fixed so that in these areas its absorption of blue matches that of the magenta dye at full concentration, i.e. is 50%. At the intermediate levels both factors come into play: as the concentration of the dye diminishes, the proportion of unused yellow coupler increases so that ideally the blue absorption of the layer remains constant throughout at 50%. Stated in another way, this means that at all concentrations the blue transmission of the dye multiplied by the blue transmission of the coupler equals 50%. Therefore variations in magenta dye concentration result, as desired, only in variations in the absorption of green. The constant blue absorption level of 50% can easily be corrected by doubling the blue constituent of the printing light, a stratagem noted above.

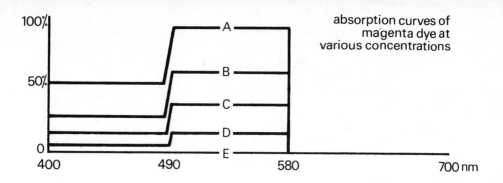

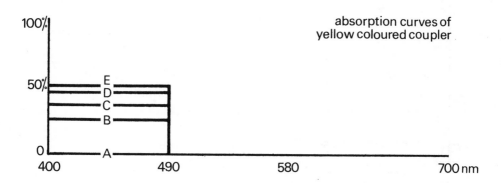

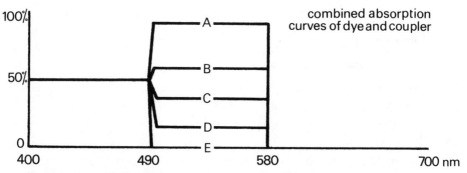

Fig. 10.2. *Diagrammatic representation of the working of a yellow coloured coupler in combination with a magenta dye*

The technique of coloured couplers has the advantage that their operation is entirely automatic, and no special processing is required. A slight loss of emulsion speed is perhaps the only disadvantage. In practice, of course, coloured couplers do not correct with as much precision as outlined above, but major improvements in colour rendition can be achieved.

After the blue absorption by magenta dyes, the second major problem is the unwanted absorption of both blue and green by cyan dyes. This may be compensated for by using a pink coupler in the red-sensitive layer.

In the negative/positive process, the absorption characteristics of subtractive dyes exert their influence on colour balance at at least two stages, first during printing and secondly during projection. If couplers of deeper colours are used, corrections may be made for both stages in the one operation. Coloured couplers cannot be incorporated in the final print film since there is no subsequent step in which compensation for the constant overall excess absorption may be made, and for the same reason they cannot be used in reversal stocks designed for projection.

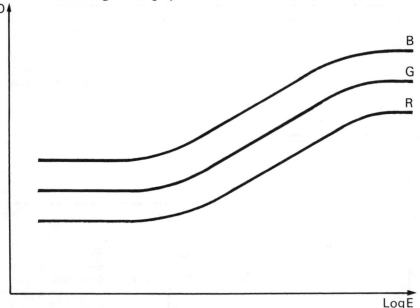

Fig. 10.3. Characteristic of a typical colour negative incorporating coloured couplers

The effect of coloured couplers may be seen in the characteristic curves of a typical colour negative (see Fig. 10.3). As may be seen, the density of the film to blue light is considerably higher than density to green, which in turn is higher than that to red. At low exposure levels, the higher densities are caused by the absorptions of the unreacted yellow and pink coloured couplers. At high exposure levels, the couplers having reacted to form dyes, the higher densities to blue and green are caused by the unwanted absorptions of the magenta and cyan dyes. The fact that the curves are separated by very nearly the same amount throughout indicates the effectiveness of the coloured coupler masking technique in maintaining excess absorptions at a constant level for any degree of exposure.

Colour Printing Using Tripack Stock

The principle of printing colour films using tripack emulsions is basically the same as that of black-and-white printing. The print film is exposed by light shone through the camera negative, reversal original or intermediate

128

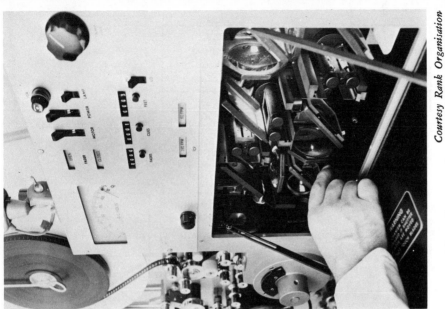

Fig. 10.5. Dichroic filter separation on an additive colour printer

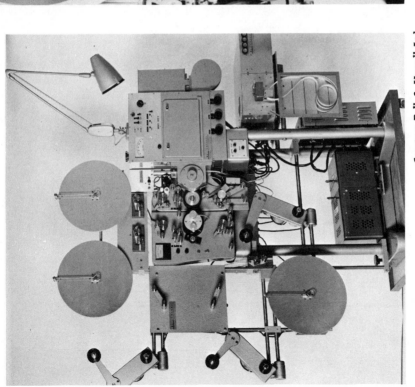

Fig. 10.4. Bell & Howell Model 6100CH additive colour printer

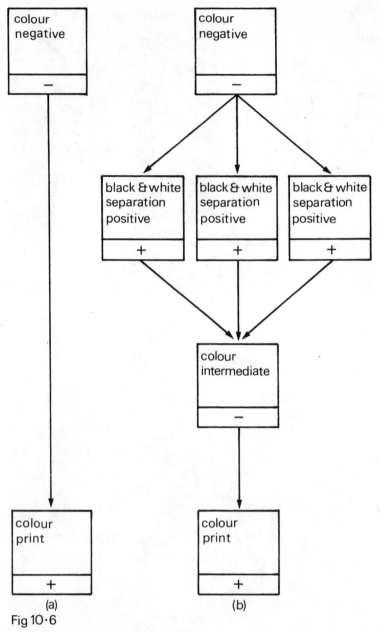

Fig 10·6

Figs. 10.6 and 10.7. Systems of release printing from colour negative and reversal originals using integral tripack stocks

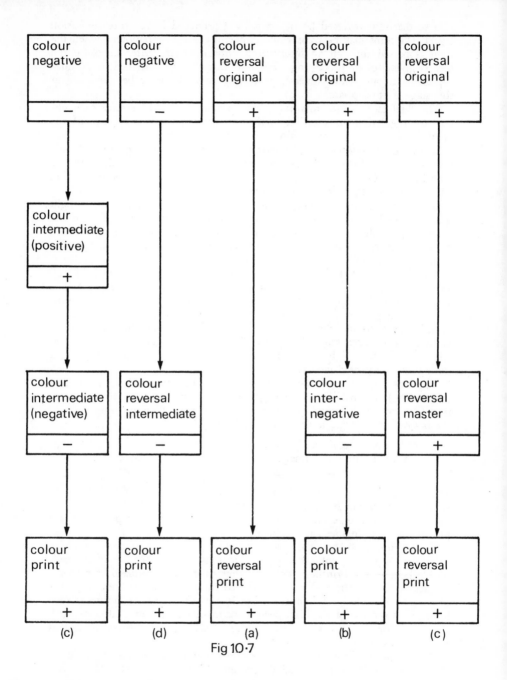

Fig 10·7

film so that tone-reversed latent images are produced in the three emulsion layers. The films may be transported either in contact or remotely, when the light is passed through an intervening optical system. After exposure the film is given colour processing similar to that already described to produce a positive colour print. Reversal processing may of course be employed at this stage if appropriate.

The chief factor differentiating colour printers is that there must be a system for regulating, in addition to the intensity, the colour balance of the printer light. There are two main techniques for doing this.

In *additive printers* the light source is divided into red, green and blue components by dichroic filters (see Fig. 8.5). The three components are then blended together in the printing gate, changes in colour balance being effected by varying their intensity in relation to each other.

In *subtractive printers* (or "white light" printers) a single white light source is used, its colour composition being varied by the insertion in the beam of pale filters of the subtractive primary colours yellow, magenta and cyan. A separate system, utilising neutral density filters or a variable aperture, regulates the overall intensity of the source.

The drawback of the subtractive technique is that the filters used, like all subtractive dyes, have subsidiary unwanted absorption characteristics. The additive method, though slightly more complicated, offers greater flexibility, better colour saturation and more accurate and consistent control of the exposures given to the three emulsion layers of the print, and is therefore gaining greater acceptance. Printers of both types are generally designed to allow shot-by-shot light changes triggered by means of punched tape or some other automated device.

The sensitising of the layers in colour print film often follows a different convention from that of camera negative stock. For maximum image sharpness it is frequently found desirable to transfer the yellow-forming layer to the bottom of the tripack, the order then being:

> MAGENTA positive dye image —top emulsion layer
> CYAN positive dye image   —middle emulsion layer
> YELLOW positive dye image   —bottom emulsion layer.

This arrangement is possible if silver chloride or silver chlorobromide emulsions, which are not sensitive to blue light, are used for the top two layers. Emulsions of this type are too slow for original shooting purposes, but for printing the loss in speed is acceptable.

Rush prints from original colour negatives sometimes present problems in evaluating photographic quality. For reasons of cost they are often made on black-and-white printing stock, and thus their use is primarily for checking action rather than the quality of the colour photography. They may also, of course, be made on colour stock but in this case they are normally one-light prints because of the highspeed work involved: density and colour balance may for this reason be misleading. Rushes may however be colour graded if desired.

Various possible methods of release printing from an original negative using tripack stock are illustrated diagrammatically in Fig. 10.6. The easiest method is that shown in (a): direct printing on to release positive stock from a colour negative. This system has its uses where only a few copies of the original are required, but as in black-and-white printing there are powerful reasons for introducing one or more intermediate steps. The most important factor is probably the danger of damage to the negative, and the lessened insurance risk when intermediate master copies are on hand. Other points are that intermediate copies facilitate reduction printing or "blowing up"; they are useful when local release printing is to be done in foreign countries; and they are necessary for some optical effects and when very large numbers of release prints are required.

A method formerly employed but now little used is that shown in (b). Printing from the colour negative on to black-and-white positive stock in three separate stages, using yellow, magenta and cyan filter packs in succession, three "separation positives" are obtained, bearing the blue, green and red records respectively. These are then printed on to a single colour intermediate negative using appropriate filters. This technique provides a high degree of control over the individual colour records but registration problems are encountered at the second printing stage. The system is now chiefly confined to special effects work, although black-and-white separation positives may also be made for long-term storage and preservation purposes.

System (c) offers an easier alternative by obviating the registration difficulties, but the employment of four colour films in successive stages results in unavoidable losses in colour quality, image sharpness and definition.

The comparatively recent introduction of colour reversal intermediate films offers a way of avoiding the drawbacks of both earlier indirect techniques, and system (d), which incorporates the new type of stock, will probably supersede (b) and (c).

As illustrated in Fig. 10.7, colour reversal original stock, used chiefly in 16mm, may be printed directly on to reversal release print stock, system (a); printed on to an "internegative" film from which the final print is produced, system (b); or printed on to a reversal master prior to release printing, which is again by reversal process, system (c). All three methods, by incorporating one or more printing stages, afford greater control over colour reproduction than can be obtained when the original is used as a projection print. The use of internegative or reversal master film offers the same advantages when more than a few copies are required as those associated with the employment of intermediate steps when printing from a colour negative.

Dye Imbibition Printing

The major alternative to tripack-stock colour printing is the system by which Technicolor release prints are made, known variously as the *relief image, dye transfer* or *dye imbibition* technique. The key to the technique is the preparation of a *dye matrix* from each of the three colour records of the original scene. The three matrices, which consist of relief images in hardened gelatin, are used to create, by means of a triple imbibition process, a colour print consisting of three transparent subtractive dye images superimposed in register on a triacetate support.

The dye matrices are produced directly from a colour negative (or colour internegative derived from a reversal original) by printing in three successive stages through filters of each primary colour in turn (see Fig. 10.8). Each matrix emulsion is appropriately colour-sensitised and suffused with a dye which tends to absorb light of the colour by which it is exposed. The

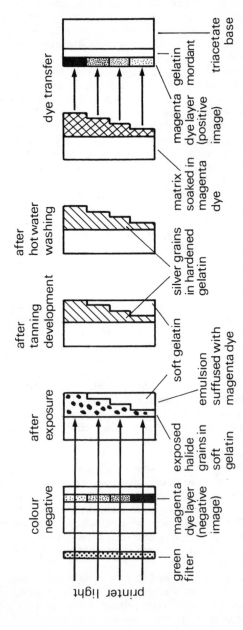

Fig. 10.8. Basic stages in the dye imbibition printing process. Cyan and yellow image layers in the print are produced in the same way.

Fig. 10.9. Matrix printer equipment

Fig. 10.10. Dye transfer equipment

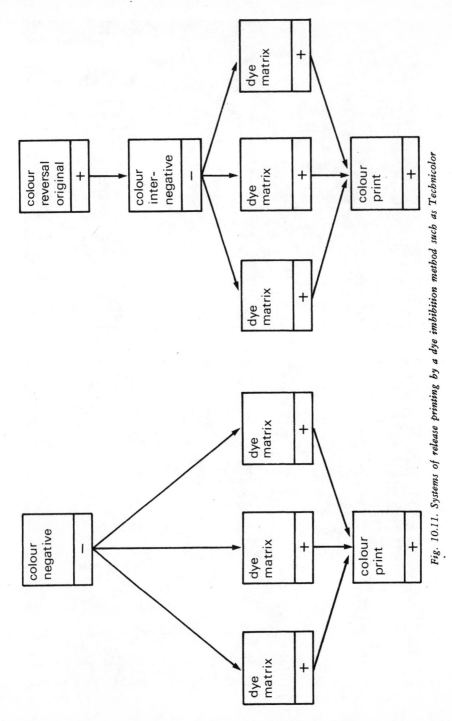

Fig. 10.11. Systems of release printing by a dye imbibition method such as Technicolor

effect of this is to impede the passage of light through the emulsion; and thus a latent image is produced which varies in *depth* according to the intensity of exposure. Printing is carried out through the film base: the parts of the emulsion furthest from the base are consequently exposed only with difficulty and a latent image at these points corresponds to the highest printer light intensity, or the darkest shadow areas in the original subject.

The film is then developed in a solution designed to harden the gelatin surrounding the exposed halide grains. This is done by using a *tanning developer* (such as pyrocatechin, pyrogallol or hydroquinone) whose oxidation products react with gelatin to render it insoluble:

$$\text{oxidised developer} + \text{gelatin} \rightarrow \text{hardened gelatin.}$$

The process resembles the formation of dyes in colour development in that the reaction takes place only in those areas where oxidised development products have been liberated, i.e. the exposed parts of the image. And similarly, the amount of sulphite in the solution must be minimal.

The next stage is washing in hot water, which dissolves away the soluble gelatin, leaving a positive relief image in which the luminance levels of the subject are reproduced by varying thicknesses of hardened gelatin instead of the usual densities of metallic silver. The matrices, each produced in this way, are then fixed and dried and may be used as the equivalent of printing plates in photo-lithography, each being soaked in dye of the appropriate complementary colour. The blue record matrix, for example, is soaked in yellow dye. The silver remaining embedded in the hardened gelatin does not impair the process and therefore is not removed. The matrices have the ability to absorb dye in proportion to the thickness of the gelatin layer and hence to the intensity of the printing exposure at that spot.

The dye-bearing matrices are then squeegeed into contact, one by one, with a gelatin-coated triacetate base, in the order magenta, cyan and yellow. The gelatin acts as a "mordant" to fix the dyes, and by transferring the dominant magenta image first maximum sharpness is obtained. It is vital that the three images are superimposed in exact register. The final print, consisting of layers of subtractive dyes, differs little in appearance from one produced by tripack methods. The same matrices may be used, by repeating the transfer process, to create very large numbers of identical release print films.

The Technicolor process can produce high quality results at comparatively low cost especially when large numbers of prints are necessary. For reasons of economy, the technique is not suitable for small quantities and a minimum print order of 40 copies from one original is usually quoted. The two basic dye imbibition printing systems, starting with colour negative and colour reversal materials respectively, are illustrated in Fig. 10.11.

Chapter XI
Colour Balance

While the eye has the ability to adapt to a wide range of illumination conditions so that the light source appears colourless (see Chapter Eight), photographic emulsions have fixed spectral sensitivity characteristics and colour film must be *balanced* to light of a particular colour temperature. Generally two classifications are found to be sufficient: films for use in artificial light, balanced for 3200°K., and those for daylight use, balanced normally for light of 5400°K.

Ideally a colour film balanced for a particular illuminant will reproduce a non-selective reflecting surface illuminated by this source as a neutral white, grey or black over a complete range of luminances. If a colour process reproduces a non-selective surface as coloured the picture is said to have a colour *cast*. A colour film exposed by light of a lower colour temperature than that for which it is balanced will have a yellowish or reddish colour cast: this is what happens e.g. when a daylight film is used for shooting in artificial light (or late afternoon sunlight) without filter correction. A colour film exposed, on the other hand, to light of a higher colour temperature than that for which it is balanced will have a bluish colour cast.

The process of balancing consists of adjusting the colour sensitivities of the three emulsion layers by varying the composition and amount of the cyanine dyes added during doctoring of the emulsion (see Chapter Two). This is a critical process which is difficult to repeat with 100% accuracy from batch to batch. Thus rolls of colour film of the same specification from the same manufacturer may vary slightly in colour balance (and also speed) if they are from different batches. To assist the cameraman a batch number is normally quoted as part of the identification data of motion picture stock, and where all the stock required for a given production cannot be obtained from the same batch, separate tests should be run and appropriate filtering and printing corrections made to compensate for any variations in the relative sensitivities of the emulsions.

Colour Temperature of Various Light Sources

The colour temperature, in degrees Kelvin, of various light sources, together with their corresponding "mired value" (explained below) are given in Table 11.1.

(a) *Artificial light sources.* It may be seen that the standard colour temperature to which colour films for artificial illumination are balanced, 3200°K., corresponds to the output of ordinary studio tungsten lamps. Adjustments (by means of filters) must be made if tungsten-halogen, photoflood or carbon arc lamps are used. It should be noted that figures given in a table such as this refer to new lamps operating at their correct voltage. Should lamps have become blackened by use, or if the voltage of the power supply is lower than normal, the colour temperature of the sources will drop. A photo-electric colour temperature meter is a valuable aid in adjudging such variations. A point to note is that variable resistance dimmers for lamps cannot be successfully used when shooting with colour film because of their effect on colour temperature.

TABLE 11.1
Colour Temperature and Mired Value
of Various Light Sources

	°K.	Mired Value
Standard candle	1930	518
Candle, approx.	2000	500
Dawn sunlight, approx.	2000	500
Domestic tungsten lamps (40–60 watt)	2800	357
Domestic tungsten lamps (100–200 watt)	2900	345
Floodlighting tungsten lamps (500 & 1000 watt)	3000	333
Warm White fluorescent lamps	3000	333
Studio tungsten lamps	3200	312
Projector tungsten lamps (500 watt)	3200	312
Tungsten-halogen lamps	3300	303
Photoflood tungsten lamps	3400	294
White fluorescent lamps	3500	286
Carbon arc	4000–6000	250–167
Cool White fluorescent ("Daylight") lamps	4300	233
Carbon arc (projector)	5000	200
Midday sunlight, approx.	5400	185
Xenon arc (projector)	5600	179
Typical average daylight	6500	154
Northlight fluorescent ("Artificial Daylight") lamps	6500	154
Overcast sky, approx.	6800	147
Hazy sky, approx.	8000	125
Clear blue sky, approx.	10,000–25,000	100–40

(b) *Daylight illumination.* Illumination on an ordinary sunny day consists of a mixture of two sources, light from the sun direct and light from the sky. Sunlight as it reaches the top layer of the earth's atmosphere has a colour temperature in the region of 6000°–7000°K. The effect of the layers of atmosphere which it then must traverse is to scatter light of the shorter wavelengths, i.e. from the blue end of the visible spectrum. Some of this light is lost into space, while the rest, after multiple diffusion, reaches the surface of the earth as blue sky light. The remaining portion of sunlight is transmitted direct and, deprived of a high proportion of its blue content, is more yellowish and thus has a lower colour temperature than sunlight as propagated through space. Actual figures vary greatly according to weather conditions, latitude, time of year, time of day, etc., but the figures of 5400°K. for midday sunlight and 6500°K. for a typical sunlight/sky light mixture represent fair approximations. It is very much more difficult to give a precise measurement for light purely from a blue sky, since this varies enormously not only with the factors already listed but also with the orientation of the sun with respect to the region of sky measured.

The lower the sun's inclination to the horizon, the thicker the band of atmosphere which the rays must traverse (see Fig. 11.1). Thus in the early morning and towards evening direct sunlight becomes much redder in con-

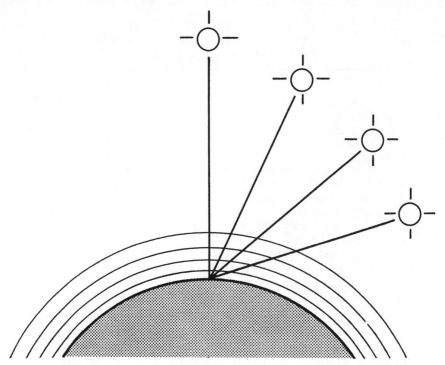

Fig. 11.1. Effect of inclination of the sun on the extent of atmospheric filtering of sunlight

tent, an effect often evident to the observer and very significant for colour photography. At sunset, in fact, the colour temperature of direct rays from the sun may be as low as 2000°K. Clearly substantial filter corrections will be needed when photographing early or late in the day if direct sunlight forms a high proportion of the illumination of the subject. Flesh tones are particularly critical in this respect and show a marked tendency to register an orange cast in such illumination conditions.

There is, however, a strong countervailing factor which comes into play whenever sky light forms a significant proportion of subject illumination, which occurs in very many photographic situations. This is that the relative intensities of sunlight and sky light in a typical daylight mixture are not constant but vary considerably according to the time of day. Thus the ratio of direct sunlight to light from a blue sky may be something like 7:1 at midday, and fall to ½:1 immediately before sunset, when sun rays are at their weakest. Diffuse light, which is of course very much bluer than sunlight, accordingly plays a more important role in general daylight illumination as an afternoon wears on, and after sunset its proportion of the total naturally reaches 100%. Filtering corrections which may be necessary at this time of day therefore depend very greatly upon the type of subject illumination: whether the subject is in shadow or receives much of its light by reflection from an indirectly illuminated surface, for example. In many cases it may be necessary to counteract excessive bluishness, rather than reddishness, late in the afternoon or, equally, in the early morning.

Clouds provide another complicating factor in estimating daylight colour temperature. Acting as non-selective diffuse reflectors, their major effect is to mix sunlight and sky light without markedly altering colour temperature. The relative amounts of the two sources in the combination reaching the earth depends on the height of the cloud layer and the extent to which it is uniform or broken up. Light from an overcast sky is generally of the order of 6800°K. and highly diffuse.

Atmospheric filtering may occasionally result in shots having an unforeseen bluish cast. One such case is objects in open shadow. In a street scene, for example, where the objects being photographed are shielded by tall buildings from sunlight either direct or reflected from nearby walls etc., the illumination may contain a very high proportion of diffuse blue sky light, though the observer, having adapted to the quality of the illumination, is not conscious of this. Another instance is distant scenes, where sunlight scattered by the atmospheric barrier intervening between the subject and the camera is mixed with light from the subject itself. This scatter light is, again, of the shorter spectral wavelengths and results in distant objects appearing bluish or even purple. The effect is obvious to an observer when the subject is at a sufficient distance, but nearer at hand—scenes photographed through a tele-photo lens at a distance of several hundred yards, for example—filtering precautions may be necessary even though the blue content of the light reaching the camera is not particularly noticeable.

Colour temperature measurements cannot be made of daylight illumination with any degree of accuracy, since the departures of daylight spectral energy curves from those of the equivalent black body are considerable. Deficiencies are most marked in the 300–450nm band, illustrating the loss of blue and ultra-violet light through reflection into space. Other irregularities are caused by absorptions in the atmospheres of both the sun and the earth.

Correcting Filters for Colour Photography

Correcting filters for use with colour film are designed to control the potential colour balance of the image. Except when special effects are being aimed at, the intention is to adjust the effective colour temperature of the illumination of the subject as it reaches the film in order to bring it in line with that to which the film is balanced, thereby helping to achieve the most naturalistic colour rendering possible. The direction of the colour temperature shift which is brought about can be judged by the colour of the filter: yellowish or reddish filters (which absorb blue light) lower the effective colour temperature of the illumination, while red-absorbing bluish or greenish filters raise it. Filters are generally placed over the camera lens. Correcting filters are sometimes divided into three classes:

(a) *Conversion (or Correction) Filters.* Conversion filters are used when a film balanced for daylight use is to be exposed by artificial light or vice versa. When it is necessary to use the same roll of film for both daylight and artificially-lit scenes, it is preferable to choose a film balanced for 3200°K. and make filter corrections for daylight shooting. This is because the amber filter required in this case has a lower filter factor, i.e. restricts film speed less, and approaches ideal spectral absorption characteristics closer than the blue filter required in the converse case.

(b) *Light-balancing Filters.* To adjust the effective colour temperature of the light source to that to which the film is balanced, light-balancing filters may be employed. Pale in colour and either yellow-brown or bluish, they are used e.g. if the lamps with which the set is lit are not rated at 3200°K., or if, though rated at 3200°K., they have a spectral output lower than this because of aging or a drop in the mains supply voltage. Another use is to make small shifts in the quality of a daylight source, but the tendency is now to leave these corrections for the laboratory to make during printing (unless of course the film is a reversal original for projection).

(c) *Colour-compensating Filters.* These are used when for some reason special compensation in the effective colour composition of the light source is required. Certain sources, for example, have significant deficiencies in their spectral energy distribution apart from considerations of overall colour temperature. Colour-compensating filters may also be used to correct for batch-to-batch variations in the colour balance of, in particular, reversal films, while another application is in underwater photography when the strong red absorption of water must be compensated for. They may be of any primary or secondary colour.

To achieve a desired effect a limited number of filters may be combined by placing them in contact together in front of the lens. Light losses caused by reflection at the interfaces and the danger of Newton's rings may be minimised by cementing the filters together.

Mixed lighting, e.g. daylight entering a room through windows combined with artificial interior lighting, presents a special problem. Obviously corrections cannot be made merely by placing a filter over the camera lens. The solution here is to filter the sources independently: in the example given, for instance, either by placing blue gelatin sheets in front of the lamps and shooting with daylight film (or tungsten film with the correct conversion filter), or by using film balanced for artificial light and placing orange sheet filters over the windows. On rare occasions, mixed lighting without filter corrections may be deliberately exploited for distinctive photographic effects.

As previously noted, corrections necessitated by photographing in light of a different colour temperature from that to which the film is balanced may be made during printing as an alternative to before-the-lens filtering, and current practice is now to leave all but major adjustments to the laboratory. Exact compensation can be made as long as none of the three emulsion layers is under- or over-exposed. In most cases where a light-balancing filter would be used, this is a reasonable assumption to make, but conversion filters cannot normally be left off when shooting without incurring the risk of mismatching of the curves and consequent ugly colour errors.

Mired Values

For accurate control of colour rendering by means of filters it is necessary to know by how much a given filter will shift the effective colour temperature of the light source. Here a complication arises. The effectiveness of a filter, measured in degrees Kelvin, is not numerically constant but is comparatively small at low colour temperature values and increases as the blue-to-red ratio of the illuminant rises. Thus the same blue filter might have the ability to raise the colour temperature of a 2000°K. source to 2100°K., and a 6000°K. source to 7000°K. Moreover, the visual effect of these two shifts, 100°K. at a lower level and 1000°K. at the higher, are approximately equivalent. It is found convenient therefore to employ a second scale which uses the reciprocal of colour temperature values in degrees Kelvin, multiplied by one million to avoid fractions. The unit of this scale, known as the *mired* (from micro-reciprocal degree), is thus given as follows:

$$\text{Mired value} = \frac{10^6}{\text{°K.}}$$

The mired value of colour temperatures are most commonly met with in cinematography is given in Table 11.2.

TABLE 11.2
Mired Value of Colour Temperature from 1000°—9900°K.

°K.	0	100	200	300	400	500	600	700	800	900
1000	1000	909	833	769	714	667	625	588	556	527
2000	500	476	455	435	417	400	385	370	357	345
3000	333	323	312	303	294	286	278	270	263	256
4000	250	244	238	233	227	222	217	213	208	204
5000	200	196	192	189	185	182	179	175	172	169
6000	167	164	161	159	156	154	152	149	147	145
7000	143	141	139	137	135	133	132	130	128	127
8000	125	123	122	120	119	117	116	115	114	112
9000	111	110	109	108	106	105	104	103	102	101

The scale approximately corresponds, in linear terms, to the absorption characteristics of filters and to the visual effect of the changing colour composition of a light source. By reference to the table, for example, it may be seen that the hypothetical filter mentioned above shifts the mired value of the source in each case by —24 units.

It is possible to designate the effectiveness of a filter by reference to its "mired-shift value." If we denote the colour temperature of the original light source by CT_1 and that of the light transmitted by the filter by CT_2, both expressed in degrees Kelvin, the formula may be given as:

$$\text{Mired-shift value} = \left(\frac{1}{CT_2} - \frac{1}{CT_1} \right) \times 10^6$$

$$= \text{Mired value } (CT_2) - \text{Mired value } (CT_1).$$

Thus, for example, the mired-shift value of a filter which converts a light source from 3600°K. to an effective colour temperature of 3200°K. is (312—278) or +34 mired. Obviously the sign of the mired-shift value is significant, in that it indicates the direction in which the shift is made: a positive mired-shift, associated with yellowish filters, increases mired value and decreases colour temperature, while a negative mired-shift, brought about by bluish filters, decreases mired value and raises colour temperature.

Using this system, calculation of colour temperature corrections may be simply made. After it has been ascertained what mired shift is required, it is only necessary to select the filter which will effect this shift according to the manufacturer's specification. The effect of several filters in combination may be calculated merely by adding their mired-shift values together, with due regard to sign. It is not normally necessary to correct closer than 100°K., and a filter or filter-combination which is within 10 mired of the theoretical ideal is found to be satisfactory.

An instrument known as a "colour correction finder" has been recently developed, designed to simplify the selection of filters required for adjusting the colour temperature of subject illumination. It is based on the principle of visual comparison of two adjacent surfaces. A reference surface in the finder is illuminated by a regulated source to a predetermined colour temperature which may be 3400°K., 3200°K., or 3000°K. Alongside this the cameraman sees, by viewing through an eyepiece, a diffusing surface illuminated by light reaching the scene to be photographed. A series of built-in filters may be interposed in graduated fashion until the colour balance of the diffusing surface exactly matches that of the reference surface. The filter required may then be read off from an indicating scale on the instrument.

Mis-Matching of Lenses and Filters

Because of chromatic aberrations etc., given lenses do not necessarily, and in fact often do not, pass light of identical colour composition. Similarly, filters may vary significantly in their absorption characteristics despite the fact that they are of the same specification. This may create serious problems of mis-matching in colour balance when, as is often the case, particularly in multi-camera setups, different lenses and filters are used on shots to be intercut in the same sequence. Since these variations may be extremely difficult to correct accurately by grading, laboratories strongly recommend that tests be run with the different lenses and filters to be used before production shooting commences.

Printing Modifications

This chapter has dealt so far with adjustments to the potential colour balance of the final image which are possible during filming. Colour processing is normally a standard procedure in which there is little room for manoeuvre, but further basic modifications in colour rendering are possible during the printing stage. Modifications may be necessary:

(a) to compensate for batch-to-batch variations in colour balance of the film stock used

(b) to compensate for shot-by-shot variations in colour rendering caused by changeable lighting conditions in location shooting

(c) to correct for misjudged filtering

(d) to make special adjustments for a particular subject matter, especially if dominated by a single colour

(e) to meet the requirements of a particular type of projection lamp or of television transmission

(f) to maintain colour continuity and make allowance for problems of successive contrast (see below)

(g) to achieve desired aesthetic effects.

As outlined in Chapter Ten, shot-by-shot colour balance adjustments may be made when printing on to integral tripack stock by modifying the relative intensities of the blue, green and red components of the printer light (in additive printers) or the combination of yellow, magenta and cyan filters in the filter pack (in subtractive printers).

A valuable aid in assessing the required colour balance for each shot is a closed circuit colour television viewing device, several models of which have

Courtesy Bell & Howell Ltd.

Fig. 11.2. Hazeltine Colour Analyser. An all-transistorised model of this machine has also recently been introduced.

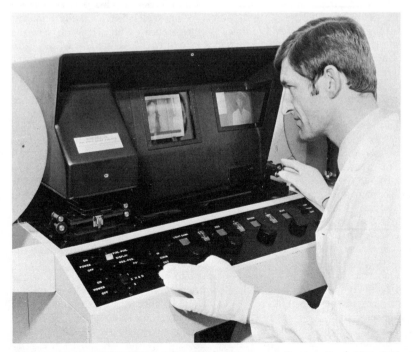

Fig. 11.3. Eastman 1635 Video Colour Analyser   *Courtesy Rank Organisation*

recently been introduced to the market. A typical video analyser of this kind electronically scans the film to be graded through blue, green and red filters in succession, the signals obtained being processed to provide an integrated positive display image in full color on a cathode ray tube. Four basic controls, regulating independently the density and the blue, green and red content of the picture, may be manipulated till the desired results are obtained. Judgement may be assisted by displaying a comparison print alongside the television tube, while the controls are calibrated directly in the numerical log exposure units used for variable printer light or filter pack settings. This type of instrument can normally be set for either negative-positive or positive-positive operation, which permits its use with reversal stocks, and in addition further adjustments are generally possible to cater for different gamma values and for the particular processing system and printer being employed on a specific run. A major advantage is that colour grading can be previewed before printing takes place.

In dye imbibition processes control of the density and colour balance of the print is exercised by variation of the printer light during preparation of the dye matrices. This determines, ultimately, the relative height of the three gelatin relief images at each point in the film. Since the required printing exposures for the blue, green and red records must be assessed independently and a separate set of printer instructions prepared for each matrix, the grading operation is slightly more complicated than with integral tripack methods.

Projection of Colour Film

The spectator watching a colour film in a darkened cinema is able to adapt quite easily to projector illumination varying widely in its colour quality. By using a flesh tone, for example, as a reference surface, the eye sees the total array of colours in the picture in approximately the same hue and saturation whether the projector lamp is e.g. a tungsten filament bulb with a colour temperature of 3200°K. or a carbon arc operating at 5000°K. However the relative lightness of different coloured areas in the picture is determined by the energy distribution of the projection source, given the densities of the print, and is largely independent of the colour quality to which observers have adapted. Thus reds for example may be up to four times as light with respect to blues if the film is projected by a tungsten lamp as compared with a carbon arc.

For this reason it is desirable that colour films be balanced in printing to the colour temperature of the light by which they are to be projected. The predominance of carbon arcs for regular theatrical projection has meant that in general 35mm release prints have been balanced to 5000°K., though the recent development of new light sources such as xenon arc discharge lamps operating at roughly 5600°K. may stimulate reconsideration of this practice. 16mm prints are generally available by request for either tungsten or arc projection.

Once the spectator has become adapted to the colour temperature of the projector light source, he develops a high degree of sensitivity to colour continuity in the film. Differences in colour balance from shot to shot may be detected with some acuity and if such changes are unintentional they may induce unpleasant sensations. This effect is occasionally seen in low-budget colour movies when the dupe footage used for opticals has not been exactly matched, in printing, to the overall colour balance of the film.

Audience sensitivity to lapses in colour continuity maximises the importance of accurate grading. In this respect consistency is more essential than realistic reproduction within individual shots considered in isolation, and this is especially so if the shots form part of the same sequence. In general, neutral surfaces should be reproduced as the same hue throughout, whether grey or with a slight colour bias.

The reproduction of colour in motion pictures may occasionally be complicated by the ability of the eye to adapt to a predominant subject colour, if it is on the screen long enough, and use it to some extent as a reference surface. If, for example, a shot or sequence is dominated by a single colour, such as green foliage or blue sea- and sky-scapes, and the eye has time to adjust, part of the predominant colour surface will be seen as grey, resulting in a desaturation of this colour and an increase in the saturation of complementary colours. Hence neutral shadows in a foliage scene, for instance, may appear pale magenta.

Successive contrast is the term used to describe the effect which occurs when adaptation of the eye to a predominant subject colour carries over from one shot to the next and affects the way in which colours are seen in the second shot. Thus following a markedly blue sequence to which the eye has adapted, a neutral grey will look yellowish for a short time, and the apparent colour balance of the picture as a whole will be correspondingly affected. If the second shot is sufficiently short, it may be printed slightly bluish in order to compensate for this.

Further complications in achieving correct colour rendering in the print arise from differences between the objective vision of the camera and the psychological and physiological subtleties of human sight. The eye, for instance, is frequently capable of distinguishing between the colour of an object and the colour of the light by which it is illuminated. Adaptation to the overall colour temperature of the light source has been discussed, but the effect occurs also in other cases. A person standing beside a red bus, for example, is illuminated to a greater or lesser extent by light which is reflected from the bus and therefore red. However the person does not look red to an observer, because there are self-adjusting mechanisms in sight to maintain colour constancy of known objects within a broad range of illumination conditions. Colour films do not have this ability: people standing by red buses, for example, show a distinct propensity for being rendered pinkish. The cameraman must beware that the colour of an object which he is photographing is not distorted by being illuminated by coloured reflected light, etc.

A further peculiarity of human colour vision is that in certain circumstances the hue of an object may appear to shift according to the intensity of its illumination. This occurs mostly, researchers have reported, in the case of small areas of a large scene which are darker than the rest, such as shadowed faces of an object. The most apparent effects are the shift of yellows toward green, and of oranges in the opposite direction, toward red. Since the phenomenon appears to be psychological, it is not recorded on film and in certain instances it may be necessary for the photographer to apply corrections by e.g. the use of coloured shadow fill light.

Chapter XII
Film for Television Transmission

A great deal of motion picture film is shot specifically for the purpose of transmission by television via *telecine* equipment. In addition, telecine is used to broadcast film originally designed for theatrical screening, and film derived from photographing a television monitor tube (*telerecording*). There are several reasons why film is often chosen in preference to video tape-recording, the alternative method. These include:

(a) Manoeuvrability of camera equipment on location

(b) Lower cost as compared with television cameras and video tape-recorders, especially for colour work

(c) Higher definition (essential if large-screen presentation is contemplated at any stage)

(d) Possibility of carrying out complicated optical effects requiring precise registration (of especial importance for television commercials)

(e) Ease of storage

(f) Ease of duplicating

(g) Compatibility of any television line, field or colour system (of great significance if programmes are to be exported).

The photographic requirements of film to be used in television transmission differ in small but significant ways from those of motion pictures for theatrical presentation. Whenever film is shot specifically for television purposes, a print is struck from an existing negative for television, or a programme is telerecorded, these must be taken into account.

Phase Inversion

An initial consideration is that, by using phase inversion circuitry, negative film may be used for transmission if desired. The technique is a simple one for black-and-white film, but is rather more complicated in the case of colour, having become practicable only through recent advances in television technology. The major advantage of using negative is that it avoids the loss of quality—in resolution, linearity of tone rendering and colour reproduction—which is unavoidable in printing on to a separate film stock. But against this must be set the serious danger of damaging the original negative, coupled with the fact that it is unadvisable to transmit film which has many splices. Moreover, the use of a camera negative severely restricts the degree to which sound dubbing, optical effects etc. may be incorporated in the film; dirt or dust on the negative is reproduced as white spots on the receiver screen; and shot-by-shot grading is not possible. In current practice, therefore, negative is generally resorted to only in cases of urgency when printing is not possible in the time available.

However in the colour film-television process the loss of quality inherent in the printing stage is such that serious consideration is being given to practicable means of utilising the original negative. One proposal involves making a positive record of the edited negative on colour videotape, which would then be replayed for transmission. Quality losses, it is suggested, could in this way be cut to a minimum, while shot-by-shot grading of colour balance and density would be possible during the transfer to magnetic tape. Electronic titling and other effects such as dissolves could also be readily carried out without a substantial sacrifice in quality. Such a method, however, has yet to be established in practice; at present colour positives are almost invariably used for television broadcasting.

Certain of the problems associated with the transmission of negatives, such as dirt specks and the complexities of colour inversion, may be averted if reversal stock is used for original shooting purposes. For this reason reversal film is often supplied to newsreel units, etc., whose footage may be urgently required. The basic dangers and difficulties connected with broadcasting an original camera film still, however, remain.

Optical and Other Effects

The characteristics of domestic cathode ray tubes impose some restriction on the types of optical and other effects which may be successfully employed in films shot for television. The long fade, often dramatically powerful in the cinema, is more likely to give a television viewer the impression that his set is malfunctioning. Likewise a complete black, between fades for example, tends to be reproduced on receivers as an overall mid-grey, and should similarly be avoided. Conversely, clear film, sometimes used to simulate flash effects, explosions, etc., may cause overloading of circuits and is therefore not recommended, a density of 0.15 above fog level being suggested as the minimum for such purposes.

Print Density Range

The greatest modification in film techniques is required to allow for the luminance range limitations of television reproduction. The average cinema screen can accommodate a luminance ratio of 40:1, and in first-class viewing conditions the figure might reach 50:1 or even more. A television screen, on the other hand, seldom attains a contrast of 20:1, taking into account the effect of stray ambient light. It can be seen that the potential for rendering shadow detail and subtle highlight tones is drastically restricted in the television process, and unless special steps are taken to limit the density range of the negative or positive print, very unpleasant compression of dark and light tones will result.

Since the television system can accommodate at the most half the luminance range possible in the cinema, the effective reduction in the density range of the transmitted film must be at least log 2, or 0.3 units. Greatest difficulty is encountered in rendering shadow tones and hence the customary aim is to lower maximum density of the television print, highlight density remaining comparatively constant. If, then, we take 2.4 as the standard maximum density of a theatrical motion picture print, it is clear that some method must be devised to reduce this figure to around 2.0 to 2.1. Three basic techniques are in fact possible:

(a) reduction of lighting contrast
(b) development of the negative and/or positive to a lower gamma
(c) reduction of printing exposure.

(a) *Reduction of lighting contrast.*

"Lighting contrast" is defined as the ratio in illumination (measured in foot-candles or lux) between the most brightly and dimly lit areas of the subject. In a conventional lighting situation, it is thus given by the ratio of key-plus-fill light to fill light alone. Lighting contrast must be clearly distinguished from the subject luminance ratio, which takes into account the reflectances of surfaces and is therefore much higher.

For television film purposes, it is recommended that the lighting contrast should normally be about 2:1, which means that lighting will be very much flatter than is usual for cinema motion picture production, particularly in black-and-white photography. The need for such a restricted lighting contrast has the practical corollary that for outdoor location photography reflectors and fill lights are vitally necessary except in the most diffuse of overcast conditions.

A further recommendation is that the reflectances of costumes and sets should be confined to values ranging between 70% and 4%. With a 2:1 lighting contrast, this implies a theoretical maximum subject luminance ratio of 35:1, actual figures in general falling considerably below this.

Examination of Fig. 12.1 reveals that restricting lighting contrast by raising fill light levels has no effect on the overall tone reproduction curve. The only

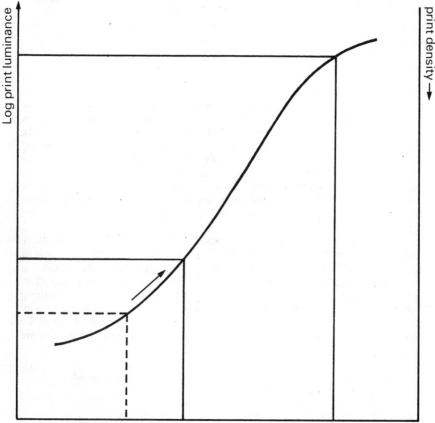

Fig. 12.1. Compression of print density range by reduction of lighting contrast

change is in the part of this curve which is used. As may be seen, luminance values no longer fall on the toe portion of the curve, with the result that the contrast as well as the luminance of shadow detail is increased. This means a distinct improvement in its visibility on the television screen.

Experience suggests that method (a) is by far the most satisfactory way of adapting to the luminance range limitations of television reproduction. Apart from the factors already discussed, the method has the advantage that no special processing is required. However particularly in the case of colour film the technique must be supplemented by other methods, and it is clearly only feasible when film is exposed specifically for television transmission.

(b) *Development of the negative and/or positive to a lower gamma.*

Some film manufacturers state that the necessary reduction in density range of the television print can be achieved, in black-and-white, solely by following the recommended restrictions in lighting contrast and reflectance range, and that normal development and printing may be carried out. With colour films, however, this is seldom the case. This is because, where a black-and-white release print may be processed to an overall reproduction gamma of 1.3, a figure of 1.6 is more usual in the case of colour materials (see Chapter Nine). In colour photography, as a result, lighting must in any event be relatively flat to confine the print density range to acceptable limits, and further compression to fulfil television requirements is not possible by alteration in lighting contrast alone. The next best is clearly to decrease the reproduction gamma.

The usual method of doing this is to print a negative processed in the regular way on to a specially-designed low contrast stock, giving it appropriate development. Television print film manufactured for this purpose has a recommended gamma of about 1.7 to 1.8, as compared with figures of 2.2 to 2.6 for normal theatrical release prints. Alternatively, it may be found that a regular release print stock may successfully be developed to the required lower contrast. In either case, achieving gamma reduction in the printing stage means that the technique can provide a basic means of deriving a print suitable for television broadcast from an existing standard motion picture negative, of a feature film, for example.

Fig. 12.2 illustrates the effect of lowering overall reproduction gamma by varying the development of the negative or positive or both. If minimum density is held constant, reduction in print luminance range is attained as desired by raising the reproduction luminance levels in shadow areas. At the same time the tone reproduction curve is flattened, i.e. the contrastiness of the print is reduced. This means that while shadow detail is brighter, its contrast is lower, an opposed effect to that produced by method (a) and one very much less likely to improve the rendering of tone variations in the darker areas of the image. Altering the gamma of the print in this way does, however, facilitate its adjustment to the overall transfer characteristics of the reproduction system (see below).

A corollary of the lower gamma attained by this method is that tolerances in grading are in general considerably higher for telecine prints than they are for cinema release prints. Since the reproduction curve is flatter, a vertical shift in the curve achieved by increasing or decreasing printing exposure by a given amount results in smaller variations in the final density range of the print.

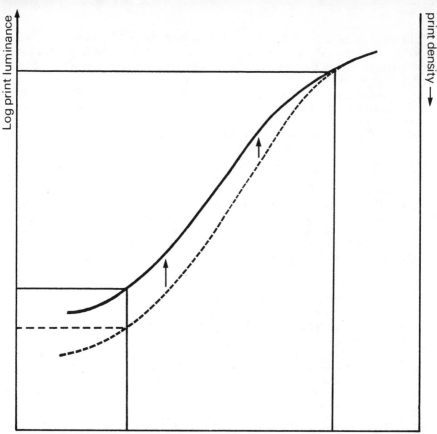

Fig. 12.2. Compression of print density range by development to a lower overall gamma

(c) *Reduction of printing exposure.*

The third possibility is to make a light print, so that the relative luminance of the final image is increased by a fixed amount at all levels except those approaching minimum density, which remains approximately constant (see Fig. 12.3). As with methods (a) and (b) the luminance of shadow detail is increased, but because gamma is only slightly reduced its contrast is virtually unchanged. The greatest drawback to this method is that, since a much wider section of the luminance range uses the shoulder of the curve, highlight tones are severely degraded. Beyond a certain point detail will in fact be entirely lost, and this factor places a definite limit on the degree of density range compression which can be obtained. These disadvantages make the technique the least advisable of the three, and it is normally employed only in rare instances when a combination of (a) and (b) fail to achieve required results.

Overall Transfer Characteristics

As was mentioned in Chapter Seven, the darker the viewing surround, the

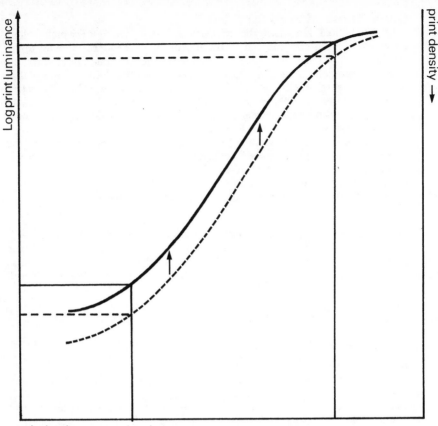

Fig. 12.3. Compression of print density range by reduction of printing exposure

lower the apparent gamma of the picture under observation. Television, viewed normally with dim ambient lighting, accordingly aims at an overall reproduction gamma intermediate between those recommended for reflection prints and cinema films, and a figure of 1.4 is becoming accepted as a norm. This is therefore the gamma value usually attained with live transmission, and when film is used in television its characteristics must be adjusted, in combination with those of the telecine apparatus, to produce an overall gamma as close to this as possible. Electronic corrections may be carried out, but in general this objective is furthered if a low contrast stock is used in accordance with method (b). A typical gamma chain for a colour film-television system is as follows:

Original Scene		Negative		Positive		Telecine		Domestic Receiver		Overall Reproduction
1.0	x	0.65	x	1.8	x	0.4	x	3.0	=	1.4

The incorporation of flare factors would reduce overall gamma and may need appropriate compensation.

Colour Balance of Films for Television

In the United Kingdom the standard reference white to which colour television pictures are balanced is Illuminant D, or 6500°K., and make-up, set decoration etc. should be determined with this in mind. As a result of viewer adaptation to the "warmer" or more reddish colours of room illumination, the television picture will tend to look rather cold: alternative reference whites of 5000°K. and 4000°K. have in fact been proposed to bring the television standard more in line with average indoor lighting. There is no universal standard in the United States.

Variations in colour balance are more noticeable on television than in the cinema and grading for colour continuity is therefore critical. For optical effects it is recommended that A and B roll printing be employed, in order to avoid the possibility of errors in colour balance caused by duplicating sections of the original. Some overall adjustment is possible electronically (see below).

Colour Errors in Television Reproduction

When filming in colour for television it is well to bear in mind the limitations of current systems of reproduction. While all types of cameras have their idiosyncracies, some errors are basic to all. The chief distortions are as follows:

GREEN — desaturated
Deep RED (towards end of spectrum) — too dark
MAGENTA — too dark, too blue
CYAN — too blue.

All dark colours are uncertain in hue and appearance.

Certain other colour imprecisions may be corrected by electronic means. These include:

(a) mis-matched *contrast* of the blue, green and red records, either through errors in film processing or through peculiarities of the telecine equipment
(b) an overall *colour cast*
(c) deficiencies in *hue* rendition, which may be corrected by techniques of electronic masking
(d) loss of *saturation*, which may be partially but seldom completely remedied, again by masking.

"Cross-colour" is a term sometimes used to describe spurious colour rendering resulting from the attempt to reproduce very fine detail. The effect arises from the receiver's misinterpreting as colour information signals carrying black-and-white detail, and may cause false blues or magentas to appear on the screen.

Fussy detail should also be avoided for other reasons. Because of the problems involved in the precise registration of the three primary images, some scrambling of colour is likely to occur particularly towards the corners of the picture if image areas are not broadly delimited. The effect of scale, in that a television screen in contrast with a cinema screen takes up only a small proportion of the viewer's angle of vision, determines in any case that minute detail should not be attempted. Finally, to avert blurring of colours at image boundaries, clear sharp contours marked by adequate contrast in lightness as well as hue are essential. This requirement also ensures that an acceptable picture will be received on compatible monochrome sets.

Bibliography

Baines, H. *The Science of Photography*. Revised by E. S. Bomback. London: Fountain Press, 1967.

Bomback, E. S. *Manual of Colour Photography*. London: Fountain Press; New York: A. S. Barnes & Co., 1964.

Corbett, D. J. *Motion Picture and Television Film: Image Control and Processing Techniques*. London and New York: Focal Press, 1968.

Duffin, G. F. *Photographic Emulsion Chemistry*. London and New York: Focal Press, 1966.

Evans, Ralph M. *Eye, Film and Camera in Color Photography*. New York: John Wiley and Sons, 1959.

Fielding, Raymond. *The Technique of Special-Effects Cinematography*. London and New York: Focal Press, 1969.

Horder, Alan (ed.). *The Ilford Manual of Photography*. Ilford: Ilford Limited, 1966.

Hunt, R. W. G. *The Reproduction of Colour*. London: Fountain Press, 1967.

James, T. H. and George C. Higgins. *Fundamentals of Photographic Theory*. New York: Morgan and Morgan; London: Fountain Press, 1960.

LaCour, Marshall and Irvin T. Lathrop. *Photo Technology*. London: Technical Press, 1966.

Langford, Michael J. *Basic Photography: A Primer for Professionals*. London and New York: Focal Press, 1965.

Lobel, L. and M. Dubois. *Basic Sensitometry*. London and New York: Focal Press, 1967.

Mason, L. F. A. *Photographic Processing Chemistry*. London and New York: Focal Press, 1966.

Mees, C. E. Kenneth. *From Dry Plates to Ektachrome Film*. New York: Ziff-Davis (A. S. Barnes), 1961.

——— and T. H. James. *The Theory of the Photographic Process*. New York: Macmillan, 1966.

Miller, Arthur C. and Walter Strenge (ed.). *American Cinematographer Manual*. Hollywood: American Society of Cinematographers, 1969.

Neblette, C. B. *Photography: Its Materials and Processes*. New York: Van Nostrand, 1963.

Society of Motion Picture and Television Engineers. *Control Techniques in Film Processing*. New York: S.M.P.T.E., 1960.

———. *Principles of Color Sensitometry*. New York: S.M.P.T.E., 1963.

Spottiswoode, Raymond (ed.). *The Focal Encyclopedia of Film and Television Techniques*. London and New York: Focal Press, 1969.

Todd, Hollis N. and Richard D. Zakia. *Photographic Sensitometry*. New York: Morgan and Morgan, 1969.

Townsend, Boris. *The Physiology and Psychology of Colour*. London: British Bureau of Television Advertising, 1969.

———. *Technical Standards of Colour Film for Television Advertising*. London: British Bureau of Television Advertising, 1969.

Wheeler, Leslie J. *Principles of Cinematography*. London: Fountain Press, 1969.

Zelikman, V. L. and S. M. Levi. *Making and Coating Photographic Emulsions*. London and New York: Focal Press, 1964.

The following periodicals will be found useful:

American Cinematographer
British Kinematography Sound and Television
Journal of the Society of Motion Picture and Television Engineers

Index

(Major references are in bold type)